WEBER'S FOOLPROOF FAVOURITES

70 simple & delicious BARBECUE RECIPES from the experts

WEBER'S
FOOLPROOF
FAVOURITES

70 simple & delicious
BARBECUE RECIPES
from the experts

hamlyn

An Hachette UK Company
www.hachette.co.uk

First published in Great Britain in 2011 by
Hamlyn, a division of Octopus Publishing Group Ltd
Endeavour House
189 Shaftesbury Avenue
London
WC2H 8JY
www.octopusbooks.co.uk

ISBN 978-0-600-62332-8

A CIP catalogue record for this book is available from the British Library

Printed and bound in China

10 9 8 7 6 5 4 3 2 1

www.weber.com®

Executive Editor: Eleanor Maxfield
Managing Editor: Clare Churly
Art Director: Jonathan Christie
Design: theoakstudio.co.uk

CONTENTS

Back in 1952, a hankering for good barbecue lit a fire under George Stephen. An employee of Weber Brothers Metal Works just outside of Chicago, George welded metal buoys for a local yacht club. But that's not all he did: George loved to grill. With a growing family at home, he found it the perfect way to relax, but couldn't find a grill on the market that lived up to his high expectations. One day, George was about to weld two buoy halves together when the idea hit: Why not use the bottom half for the cooking bowl, and the top half for the lid to create a grill? Piece by piece, his vision started coming together. He then added a handle and three legs and took his crazy-looking contraption home to test. As the story goes, when George first tried out his prototype, it didn't work quite as hoped. No matter how hard he tried, it just wouldn't stay lit. A neighbour peering over the back fence offered a little friendly advice, 'Poke some holes in that thing so the fire can get some air!' So George did, and the flames of invention could finally keep burning. He hit the road, demonstrating his funny looking creation at stores across the country. And the rest, as they say, is history. Since then Weber have strived to develop the very best in barbecue products, accessories and recipes. Weber's expertise has helped generations to enjoy a foolproof food experience. Whether on gas or charcoal the results are the same – perfect food every time.

Today you can visit Weber Grill Academies in all corners of the world, set up so you can experience one-on-one expert tuition for all your barbecue needs whether it's learning the basics or perfecting a masterclass skill. See the back page for details of the UK Weber Grill Academy where you, too, can learn to barbecue the foolproof way. In this book you'll find over 70 recipes which are guaranteed to deliver. We've chosen a range of inspirational dishes that cover the basic cuts of meat as well as giving you a few clever ideas for dishes you might never think of cooking on your barbecue. What all the recipes have in common is a triple-tested method that is easy to follow.

FOOLPROOF FAQs

Troubleshoot with the experts to ensure you get perfect results every time.

Q: What's the difference between cooking over a wood fire versus a charcoal fire? Is one better than the other?

A: Wood fire imparts a wonderful flavour, but it tends to create huge amounts of smoke and often requires waiting up to an hour or more for the flames to settle down and the embers to reach a manageable level of heat. Charcoal will reach ideal temperatures faster than wood and with much less smoke, good quality charcoal briquettes will also last a lot longer. Why not add a small amount of soaked wood chips to your lit charcoal to provide a more smoky flavour.

Q: What about briquettes? How are they different from lump charcoal?

A: We recommend using briquettes rather than lumpwood charcoal (lumpwood charcoal is raw charcoal or natural charcoal). Lumpwood charcoal tends to burn very hot and too quickly. Briquettes will perform better in your charcoal barbecue for superior cooking results. You may not think there's a difference between briquettes, but there is! Good quality briquettes such as those from Weber® are made from high purity carbon concentrate derived from mineral coal, light easily, maintain a steady cooking temperature, and burn longer than other brands. Other brands may contain fillers that make lighting difficult, then burn out quickly to gritty ash.

Q: What's the best way to get started?

A: Actually there are a few tricks, and any one of them will help: using the right charcoal, using Fire Lighter Cubes, and using a 'Chimney Starter'.

Charcoal: First, start with good-quality charcoal briquettes

Lighter cubes: Second, to light briquettes safely and with minimum hassle, try paraffin-based firelighters such as Weber® fire starters. These solid fuel cubes light as easily as a birthday candle (even when wet!) and are odourless and non-toxic, leaving no residue to mar the flavour of your delicious grilled meal.

Chimney Starter: The Chimney Starter holds the charcoal briquettes in a cylinder for fast, easy lighting. Fill the canister-shaped starter with the proper amount of charcoal, place on the charcoal grate over two or three fire lighter cubes or crumpled newspaper, ignite the cubes or paper, and let the coals burn until they have a coating of light grey ash (about 25 to 30 minutes). Pour the hot coals onto the charcoal grate and arrange for 'grilling' (direct cooking) or 'roasting' (indirect cooking) with long-handled tongs. For safety's sake, wear barbecue mitts.

Q: Are you saying I shouldn't use lighter fluid?

A: Yes, that's right. Lighter fluid is a petroleum based product that can really ruin the flavour of your food.

Q: How much charcoal should I use?

A: It depends on the size of your barbecue and how much food you want to cook. Let's assume you have a classic 57-cm (22½-inch) diameter kettle barbecue and you are cooking for four to six people. The simplest way to measure the right amount of coal is to use your chimney starter. Use it like a measuring cup for charcoal. Filled to the rim (about 80 to 100 standard briquettes) it will provide enough charcoal to spread a single, tightly packed layer across about two-thirds of the charcoal grate. That's usually enough charcoal to grill a couple of courses for four to six people.

Q: What's the process for lighting a gas barbecue?

A: Every gas barbecue will be different, so be sure to consult the owner's manual that came with your barbecue. To light a Weber® gas barbecue, first open the lid so unlit gas fumes don't collect in the cook box. Next, making sure that the control knob(s) are in the off position, slowly open the valve on your propane tank. Then turn on the first burner to the start/high setting. Push the ignition button until you hear it spark. Check that the burner is lit by looking through the matchlight hole on the front or side of the cook box. You should see a flame. Once burner one is lit you can light burner two and three etc. Close the lid and preheat the barbecue for 10 to 15 minutes.

Q: What if I smell gas?

A: If you suspect gas is escaping from the barbecue including the hose and regulator connection turn OFF the gas. DO NOT OPERATE THE GRILL and contact your local dealer or manufacturer. If you suspect it is escaping from the liquid propane tank, disconnect the hose from the tank if it's still connected to the barbecue. Move the tank away from the house or anything combustible and call your liquid propane dealer or the tank manufacturer and follow their recommendations on how to correct the problem.

Q: What exactly is the difference between 'direct heat' (grilling) and 'indirect heat' (roasting)?

A: Direct cooking (grilling) is simply grilling foods directly over the heat source. For indirect cooking (roasting) the heat source is placed to the side of the food, not directly under it. As a general rule, foods that take less than 25 minutes to cook, like boneless chicken breasts, pork chops, and steak are barbecued by the 'grilling' or direct method.

Foods that require longer cooking times at lower temperatures, like whole chicken and roasts, should be barbecued by the 'roasting' or indirect method. You can use either method on both Weber® charcoal barbecues and Weber® gas barbecues. For complete instructions, visit www.weberbbq.co.uk

If you like to barbecue, you are going to love this app!

Weber's On The Grill features loads of classic Weber recipes plus plenty of ideas for rubs, marinades and sauces that are sure to get you fired up to get out and get barbecuing.

You can tag your favourites, and even create and share a master shopping list for your recipes. There's a timer within the app, too, so you know exactly when to take your food off the barbecue.

Available to download on the UK App Store

9

Indonesian
LAMB SATAY
with SPICY
PEANUT SAUCE

prep **30*** mins

bbq **3–4** mins

serves **4**

skill ★★☆

*marinating: 30–60 mins

Special equipment: bamboo skewers, soaked in water for at least 30 minutes

MARINADE

- 1 large garlic clove, crushed
- 1 star anise
- 2 tablespoons vegetable oil
- 1 tablespoon finely chopped fresh ginger
- 1 tablespoon fresh lime juice
- 1 tablespoon soy sauce
- 1 teaspoon chilli powder

- 2 lamb fillets, each about 250 g (8 oz), trimmed of excess fat and sinew

SAUCE

- 1 tablespoon vegetable oil
- 1 teaspoon Thai red curry paste
- 1 teaspoon ground cumin
- 1 teaspoon dried lemongrass
- 125 g (4 oz) smooth peanut butter
- 125 ml (4 fl oz) coconut milk
- 1 tablespoon soy sauce
- 1 teaspoon fresh lime juice
- 1 teaspoon granulated sugar

1 Combine the marinade ingredients in a food processor or blender and process until smooth.

2 Cut the lamb fillets crossways (against the grain) into 1-cm (½-inch) slices. Place the slices in a large, resealable plastic bag and pour in the marinade. Press the air out of the bag and seal tightly. Turn the bag several times to distribute the marinade, place the bag in a bowl, and marinate at room temperature for 30 minutes or in the refrigerator for 1 hour, turning occasionally.

3 Warm the vegetable oil in a medium sauté pan over a medium high heat. Add the red curry paste, cumin and lemongrass, stirring to release their fragrance for about 10 seconds. Add the peanut butter, coconut milk and 125 ml (4 fl oz) of water. Mix well. Add the soy sauce, lime juice and sugar. Stir. Lower the heat to a simmer and cook for 1–2 minutes. Set aside.

4 Prepare the grill for grilling over high heat (230–290°C/450–550°F).

5 Remove the lamb from the bag and discard the marinade. Thread the lamb slices lengthways on the skewers. Just before you grill the lamb, gently reheat the sauce; whisk in a little coconut milk or water, if needed, to thin it. Brush the cooking grates clean. Grill the lamb over high grilling heat for 3–4 minutes, with the lid closed as much as possible and turning once. Remove from the grill and serve hot with the sauce.

JERK
PRABWNS

prep
- 15* -
mins

bbq
- 2–4 -
mins

serves
4–6

skill
★☆☆

*marinating: 30–45 mins

Special equipment: 12 bamboo skewers, soaked in water for at least 30 minutes

MARINADE
- 1 onion, roughly chopped
- 1 jalapeño chilli, roughly chopped
- 3 tablespoons white wine vinegar
- 2 tablespoons soy sauce
- 2 tablespoons rapeseed oil
- ½ teaspoon Tabasco sauce
- ½ teaspoon ground allspice
- ¼ teaspoon garlic granules
- ¼ teaspoon ground cinnamon
- ¼ teaspoon sea salt
- ¼ teaspoon freshly ground black pepper
- ⅛ teaspoon ground nutmeg

- 1 kg (2 lb) large prawns, peeled and deveined
- 1 lime, cut into wedges

1 Combine the marinade ingredients in a food processor. Process until smooth.

2 Put the prawns in a large, resealable plastic bag and pour in the marinade. Press out the air and seal the bag tightly. Turn the bag to distribute the marinade and refrigerate for 30–45 minutes.

3 Prepare the grill for grilling over high heat (230–290°C/450–550°F).

4 Remove the prawns from the bag and discard the marinade. Thread the prawns on to the skewers through both the heads and tails.

5 Brush the cooking grates clean. Grill the prawns over high grilling heat for 2–4 minutes, with the lid closed as much as possible and turning once, until the prawns are firm to the touch and just turning opaque in the centre. Place on a serving platter, squeeze a little lime juice over the prawns and serve warm.

Marinated Mushroom
BRUSCHETTA
with PINE NUTS
and GOATS' CHEESE

prep
45*
mins

bbq
21–27
mins

serves
6–8

skill
★★☆

*marinating: 1–2 hours

MARINADE
- 125 ml (4 fl oz) dry white wine
- 4 tablespoons extra-virgin olive oil
- 2 teaspoons finely chopped garlic
- 2 teaspoons finely chopped fresh rosemary
- ½ teaspoon sea salt
- ¼ teaspoon freshly ground black pepper

- 250 g (8 oz) large shiitake mushrcoms, stems removed
- 2 red peppers
- 20 slices good-quality French bread, each about 5 cm (2 inches) in diameter and 5mm (¼ inch) thick
- Extra-virgin olive oil
- 25 g (1 oz) pine nuts
- 15 g (½ oz) flat leaf parsley, finely chopped
- 125 g (4 oz) goats' cheese

1 Whisk the marinade ingredients in a medium bowl. Place the mushrooms in a large, resealable plastic bag and pour in the marinade. Press the air out of the bag and seal tightly. Turn the bag several times to distribute the ingredients. Allow the mushrooms to marinate at room temperature for 1–2 hours, turning the bag occasionally.

2 Prepare the grill for grilling over medium heat (180–230°C/350–450°F).

3 Brush the cooking grates clean. Grill the peppers over medium grilling heat for 12–15 minutes, with the lid closed as much as possible and turning occasionally, until they are blackened and blistered all over. Place the peppers in a medium bowl and cover with clingfilm to trap the steam. Set aside for at least 10 minutes, then peel the skins and discard the stems and seeds.

4 Shake any excess moisture from the mushrooms. Grill them over medium grilling heat for 8–10 minutes, turning occasionally, until tender. Lightly brush the slices of bread on both sides with olive oil. Grill over medium grilling heat for 1–2 minutes, turning once, until lightly toasted.

5 Cook the pine nuts in a medium sauté pan over a medium heat for 5–10 minutes, shaking the pan occasionally, until lightly toasted.

6 Finely chop the peppers, mushrooms and pine nuts, and combine all of them in a medium bowl. Add the parsley and stir. Spread a very thin layer of goats' cheese on one side of each slice of bread. Arrange about 1 tablespoon of mushroom mixture on top of each. Serve at room temperature.

Thin-Crusted
PIZZAS
with Grilled Red Onions and Black Olives

prep 45 mins | bbq 15–20 mins | serves 4–6 | skill ★☆☆

DOUGH

- 1 sachet dried yeast
- ½ teaspoon granulated sugar
- 175 ml (6 fl oz) warm water (40–46°C/105–115°F)
- 375 g (12 oz) plain flour, plus more for rolling dough
- 3 tablespoons extra-virgin olive oil
- 1 teaspoon sea salt

SAUCE

- 2 tablespoons extra-virgin olive oil
- 1 small red onion, finely chopped
- 2 teaspoons finely chopped garlic
- 1 teaspoon dried oregano
- 750-g (28-oz) can whole tomatoes
- ½ teaspoon granulated sugar
- ½ teaspoon sea salt
- ¼ teaspoon freshly ground black pepper

- 2 large red onions, cut crossways into 8-mm (⅓-inch) slices
- Extra-virgin olive oil
- 50 g (2 oz) Mediterranean black olives, pitted and cut in half
- 250 g (8 oz) mozzarella cheese, grated
- 15 g (½ oz) flat leaf parsley, finely chopped

1 Combine the yeast and sugar with the warm water in a medium bowl. Stir once and let stand for 5–10 minutes until foamy. Add the flour, olive oil and the salt. Stir until the dough holds together. Transfer to a lightly floured work surface and knead for 4–6 minutes until smooth. Shape into a ball and place in a lightly oiled bowl. Turn the ball to cover the surface with oil. Cover the bowl with clingfilm and set aside in a warm place for 1–1½ hours until the dough doubles in size.

2 Warm the olive oil in a medium saucepan over a medium-high heat. Add the onion and cook for about 5 minutes until soft, stirring occasionally. Add the garlic and oregano, and cook for about 1 minute until the garlic is light brown, stirring occasionally. Add the tomatoes, including the juice. Use the back of a large spoon to crush the tomatoes. Season with the sugar, salt and pepper. Bring the sauce to the boil, and then lower the heat to a simmer. Cook for 40–45 minutes, stirring occasionally, until you have 475 ml (16 fl oz) of sauce. Let cool slightly and then purée in a food processor or blender. Allow to cool.

3 Prepare the grill for griling over medium heat (180–230°C/350–450°F).

4 Lightly brush the onion slices with oil. Brush the cooking grates clean. Grill the onion slices over medium grilling heat for 10–12 minutes, with the lid closed as much as possible and turning once, until well marked and tender. Remove from the grill and cut each slice in half.

5 Punch down the dough in the bowl. Transfer to a lightly floured surface and cut into four equal pieces. Cut baking paper into four 23-cm (9-inch) squares and lightly oil each sheet of paper on one side. Roll or press the dough flat on

18

the oiled side of the paper into circles about 20 cm (8 inches) in diameter, leaving the dough a little thicker at the edges than in the middle. Then lightly oil the top side of each dough round.

6 Brush the cooking grates clean. Lay the rounds on the cooking grate, with the paper sides facing up. Grab one corner of the paper with tongs and peel off. Bake the rounds over medium heat for 2–3 minutes, with the lid closed as much as possible and rotating the pizza bases occasionally for even cooking, until they are marked on the underside. Don't worry if the crusts bubble; they will deflate when turned over. Transfer the bases to the back of a roasting tray, with the grilled sides facing up.

7 Spread about 125 ml (4 fl oz) of the sauce across each pizza base, leaving a 1-cm (½-inch) border around the edges. Arrange the onions and olives over the sauce. Sprinkle the cheese on top. Transfer the pizzas from the roasting tray to the cooking grate. Bake over medium heat for 4–5 minutes, with the lid closed as much as possible and rotating the pizzas occasionally for even cooking, until the crusts are crisp and the cheese is melted. Transfer to a chopping board. Garnish with parsley. Cut into wedges and serve warm.

Chicken

prep **15*** mins | bbq **30–50** mins | serves **4** | skill ★★☆

*marinating: 4–6 hours (or up to 12 hours)

MARINADE

- 5 large spring onions, cut into 2.5-cm (1-inch) pieces
- 125 g (4 oz) basil
- 3 large garlic cloves
- 2 serrano chillies, roughly chopped
- 4 tablespoons extra-virgin olive oil
- 2 tablespoons sherry vinegar
- 1 teaspoon sea salt
- ½ teaspoon freshly ground black pepper

- 2–2.5 kg (4–5 lb) whole chicken
- Basil leaves, to garnish

1 Combine the marinade ingredients in a food processor or blender and process for 1–2 minutes to form a smooth paste.

2 Cut the chicken into six pieces: two breast pieces, two legs with thighs and two wings (remove and discard the wing tips). Then cut the legs through the joint between the drumsticks and thighs. Cut each half breast in half crossways. Place the chicken pieces in a large, resealable plastic bag and pour in the marinade. Press the air out of the bag and seal it tightly. Turn the bag several times to distribute the marinade, place the bag in a bowl and refrigerate for 4–6 hours, or as long as 12 hours, turning the bag occasionally.

3 Prepare the grill for grilling and roasting over medium heat (180–230°C/350–450°F).

4 Remove the chicken pieces from the bag and discard the marinade. Brush the cooking grates clean. Roast the chicken, skin side down, over medium roasting heat, with the lid closed, until fully cooked. The breast and wing pieces will take 30–40 minutes. The leg and thigh pieces will take 40–50 minutes. For crispier skin, grill the chicken over medium grilling heat during the last 5–10 minutes of cooking time. Garnish with basil leaves and serve warm.

Ham and Mozzarella 'Sandwiches'

- 2 red peppers
- Extra-virgin olive oil
- 1 teaspoon sea salt
- ¼ teaspoon freshly ground black pepper
- 2 large rounded aubergines, about 500 g (1 lb) each, trimmed
- 8 thin slices Parma ham
- 8 slices mozzarella, each 5 mm (¼ inch) thick
- 8 basil leaves

1 Prepare the grill for grilling over medium heat (180–230°C/350–450°F).

2 Brush the cooking grates clean. Grill the peppers over medium grilling heat for 12–15 minutes, with the lid closed as much as possible and turning occasionally, until they are blackened and blistered all over. Place the peppers in a medium bowl and cover with clingfilm to trap the steam. Set aside for at least 10 minutes, then peel the skin and discard the stems and seeds. Place the peppers in a food processor with 1 tablespoon oil and the salt and pepper. Process until smooth, scraping down the sides as needed.

3 Cut each aubergine crossways into eight slices, each about 1 cm (½ inch) thick. Lightly brush both sides with oil. Grill over medium grilling heat for 3–4 minutes, with the lid closed, until the underside is well marked. Transfer half of the slices to a roasting tray, with the grilled sides facing up. Turn the remaining slices over and grill for a further 3–4 minutes until well marked on both sides.

4 Place a tablespoon of the red pepper mixture in the centre of the grilled side of each aubergine slice on the roasting tray. Place a slice of Parma ham (folded to fit), a slice of the mozzarella and a basil leaf on top of the red pepper mixture. Top each 'sandwich' with a slice of the aubergine that has been grilled on both sides. Use a fish slice to place the 'sandwiches' on the cooking grate, uncooked side down, and grill over medium grilling heat for 2–3 minutes, until the cheese is softened and the sandwiches are heated through. Serve warm with the remaining pepper mixture, if liked.

and Hot Italian Sausage Kebabs

prep 20 mins

bbq 4–6 mins

serves 4

skill ★☆☆

Special equipment: 8 bamboo skewers, soaked in water for at least 30 minutes

- 4 hot Italian sausages, about 375 g (12 oz) total weight
- 1 red onion
- 2 tablespoons extra-virgin olive oil
- 4 tablespoons water
- 2 tablespoons white wine vinegar
- ½ teaspoon dried oregano
- ¼ teaspoon sea salt
- ⅛ teaspoon freshly ground black pepper
- 500 g (1 lb) large scallops, each about 25 g (1 oz)

1 Use a fork to pierce the sausages in several places and put them in a large frying pan. Cut the onion into quarters through the stem end. Cut each quarter in half crossways. Add the onions to the pan along with 1 tablespoon of the oil and the water. Bring to the boil over a high heat. Lower the heat to medium and cook for 10–12 minutes, turning the sausages and onions occasionally, until the water has evaporated and the juices from the sausages are browning in the pan. Remove the sausages and onions. Add the vinegar to the pan and stir to scrape up the brown crusty bits. Pour the brown bits and vinegar into a medium bowl. Add the remaining 1 tablespoon of oil, the oregano, salt and pepper.

2 Prepare the grill for grilling over medium heat (180–230°C/350–450°F).

3 Rinse the scallops and pat dry. Remove the small tough side muscle from any scallops that still have it. Add the scallops to the vinegar mixture and toss to coat. Cut the sausages into 2.5-cm (1-inch) pieces. Thread the scallops and sausages through their sides onto skewers, alternating them with pieces of onion.

4 Brush the cooking grates clean. Grill the kebabs over medium grilling heat for 4–6 minutes, with the lid closed as much as possible and turning once, until the scallops and sausages are browned and cooked through. Serve warm.

Rustic
WHITE BEAN
SOUP

prep **20** mins | bbq **10–12** mins | serves **4** | skill ★☆☆

- 1 large onion, cut into 1-cm (½-inch) slices
- 8 large ripe plum tomatoes, cored
- 2 tablespoons extra-virgin olive oil, plus more for brushing the onions and tomatoes
- 1 teaspoon finely chopped garlic
- 2 x 475-g (15-oz) cans cannellini beans
- 50 g (2 oz) basil, coarsely chopped
- Sea salt
- Freshly ground black pepper
- 2 teaspoons balsamic vinegar

1 Prepare the grill for grilling over high heat (230–290°C/450–550°F).

2 Lightly brush the onion slices and tomatoes with olive oil. Brush the cooking grates clean. Grill the onion slices over high grilling heat for 10–12 minutes, with the lid closed as much as possible and turning once, until lightly charred on both sides. At the same time, grill the tomatoes over high grilling heat for 3–5 minutes, turning occasionally, until the skins are loosened and lightly charred on all sides. Set aside.

3 Peel and discard the loosened skins from the tomatoes. Roughly chop the tomatoes and onions. Warm the olive oil in a large saucepan over a medium-high heat. Add the garlic and grilled onions and cook for 2 minutes, stirring occasionally. Add the grilled tomatoes, cannellini beans (with their liquid) and basil. Season with salt and pepper. Bring to the boil, then simmer for 10 minutes, stirring occasionally. Adjust seasoning, if necessary. Add the balsamic vinegar, give the soup a final stir and serve.

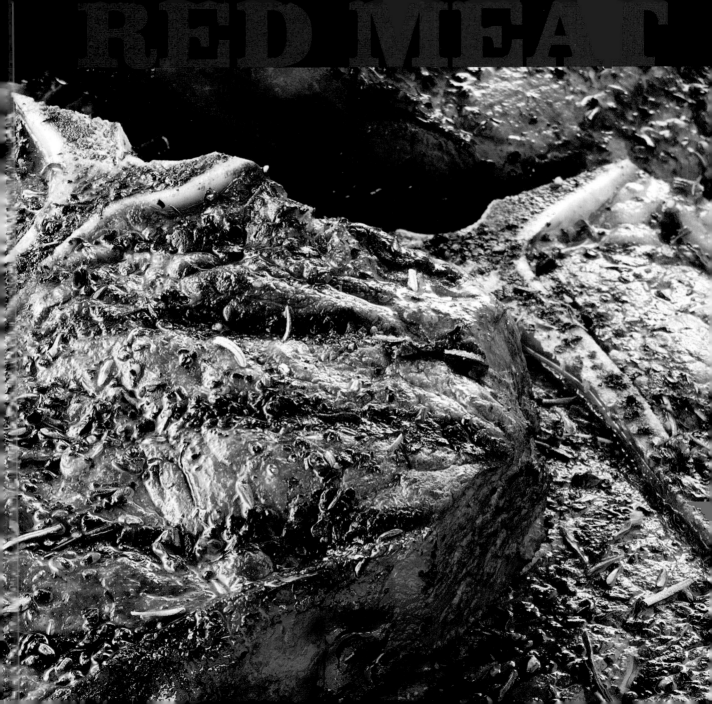

RACK OF LAMB
with ROASTED SHALLOT VINAIGRETTE

prep 15 mins | bbq 17–19 mins | serves 4 | skill ★★★

VINAIGRETTE

- 1 large unpeeled shallot, about 25 g (1 oz)
- 4 tablespoons extra-virgin olive oil
- 1 tablespoon balsamic vinegar
- 1 teaspoon Dijon mustard
- 1 teaspoon finely chopped thyme
- ½ teaspoon sea salt
- ¼ teaspoon freshly ground black pepper

- 2 racks of lamb, each 500–750 g (1 lb–1 lb 8 oz), frenched
- Extra-virgin olive oil
- 15 g (½ oz) thyme, finely chopped
- ½ teaspoon sea salt
- ½ teaspoon freshly ground black pepper

1 Prepare the grill for grilling and roasting over medium heat (180–230°C/350–450°F).

2 Lightly brush the shallot all over with some of the olive oil. Brush the cooking grates clean. Grill the shallot over medium grilling heat for about 15 minutes, with the lid closed as much as possible and turning once, until it is blackened in spots and very soft throughout. Remove the shallot from the grill and allow to cool. Remove and discard the peel. Finely chop the shallot and put it in a medium bowl along with the remaining vinaigrette ingredients, whisking in the rest of the olive oil to create a smooth dressing.

3 Trim any excess fat from the lamb. Allow to stand at room temperature 20–30 minutes before grilling. Lightly brush or spray the lamb with oil and season with the thyme, salt and pepper. Loosely cover the bones with aluminium foil to keep them from burning. Sear, bone side down first, over medium grilling heat for 2–4 minutes, with the lid closed as much as possible and turning once, until lightly browned (flare-ups might occur). Move the lamb over medium roasting heat, close the lid, and cook to your desired doneness, about 15 minutes more for medium rare. Remove from the grill and let rest for 5 minutes before cutting into chops. Serve warm with the vinaigrette.

LAMB BURGERS
with Oregano, Mint and Cucumber-Garlic Sauce

prep 15 mins • bbq 8–10 mins • serves 6 • skill ★☆☆

SAUCE

- 125 g (4 oz) cucumber
- 2 teaspoons finely chopped garlic
- 50 g (2 oz) mint, finely chopped
- 125 g (4 oz) plain yogurt
- ½ teaspoon sea salt
- Few drops Tabasco sauce

BURGERS

- 1 kg (2 lb) minced lamb
- 100 g (3-½ oz) feta cheese, crumbled
- ½ onion, finely chopped
- 15 g (½ oz) oregano, finely chopped
- 1½ teaspoons sea salt
- ½ teaspoon freshly ground black pepper
- 6 burger buns
- 6 slices ripe tomato

1 Peel and grate the cucumber. Drain in a colander while preparing the rest of the ingredients. Combine the garlic, a quarter of the mint, the drained cucumber and the remaining sauce ingredients in a small bowl. Cover and refrigerate until ready to serve.

2 Gently mix the burger ingredients, including the remaining chopped mint, in a large bowl. Shape the meat into six burgers of equal size, about 1.5 cm (¾ inch) thick. Refrigerate for at least 15 minutes before grilling.

3 Prepare the grill for grilling over high heat (230–290°C/450–550°F).

4 Brush the cooking grates clean. Grill the burgers over high grilling heat for 8–10 minutes, with the lid closed as much as possible and turning once, until cooked through. During the last 30 seconds, toast the buns, cut side down, over grilling heat.

5 Serve the lamb burgers on the toasted buns with tomato slices and cucumber sauce.

MOROCCAN
LAMB

prep **30** mins · bbq **8–10** mins · serves **4** · skill ★★☆

SEASONING MIX
- ½ teaspoon sea salt
- ½ teaspoon ground ginger
- ¼ teaspoon ground cumin
- ¼ teaspoon turmeric
- ¼ teaspoon ground cinnamon
- ¼ teaspoon ground allspice
- ¼ teaspoon freshly ground black pepper
- ¼ teaspoon ground cardamom
- ⅛ teaspoon crumbled saffron threads

- 625 g (1 lb 4 oz) minced lamb

SAUCE
- 175 g (6 oz) plain yogurt
- 25 g (1 oz) red onion, finely chopped
- 1 tablespoon finely chopped dill
- 1 tablespoon finely chopped mint
- 1 tablespoon fresh lime juice
- 1 tablespoon extra-virgin olive oil
- ½ teaspoon freshly ground black pepper
- ¼ teaspoon sea salt

- Extra-virgin olive oil
- 4 pitta breads
- 40 g (1½ oz) torn lettuce leaves
- 125 g (4 oz) tomatoes, diced

1 Combine the seasoning mix ingredients in a small heavy-based sauté pan and cook over a medium heat for about 1 minute, stirring, until fragrant. Remove from the heat.

2 Combine the lamb with the seasoning mix and 3 tablespoons cold water in a large bowl. Lightly mix with your hands; don't overwork the meat. With wet hands, lightly shape the meat into four equal-sized burgers, each about 1.5 cm (¾ inch) thick. Cover and refrigerate until ready to grill.

3 Just before grilling the burgers, make the sauce. Whisk all the sauce ingredients together in a small bowl.

4 Prepare the grill for grilling over medium heat (180–230°C/350–450°F).

5 Brush the cooking grates clean. Lightly brush or spray the lamb burgers with olive oil. Grill over medium grilling heat for 7–9 minutes, with the lid closed as much as possible and turning once, until the lamb is cooked to medium doneness. Grill the pitta breads over grilling heat for 30–60 seconds, turning once, until toasted.

6 Slip the lamb burgers inside the pitta breads along with a heaped spoonful of the yogurt sauce. Top with the lettuce and tomato. Serve immediately.

Double-Cut
LAMB CHOPS
with Cucumber-Yogurt Sauce

prep **25** mins — bbq **10** mins — serves **4** — skill ★☆☆

SAUCE

- 7.5-cm (3-inch) piece cucumber, peeled and cut into 5-mm (¼-inch) dice
- 4 spring onions (white part only), finely chopped
- 1 tablespoon fresh lemon juice
- 250 g (8 oz) plain yogurt
- 1 tablespoon extra-virgin olive oil
- 1 tablespoon finely chopped dill
- ⅛ teaspoon paprika
- Sea salt
- Freshly ground black pepper

- 1 tablespoon fresh lemon juice
- 3 tablespoons extra-virgin olive oil
- 2 teaspoons finely chopped oregano
- 2 teaspoons finely chopped garlic
- ½ teaspoon sea salt
- ¼ teaspoon freshly ground black pepper
- 8 double lamb chops, 2.5–3 cm (1–1¼ inches) thick, trimmed of nearly all fat

1 Combine the sauce ingredients in a medium bowl, including salt and pepper to taste.

2 Whisk the lemon juice, olive oil, oregano, garlic, salt and pepper in a small bowl. Brush the lamb chops with the olive oil mixture and marinate at room temperature for 10 minutes.

3 Prepare the grill for grilling over medium heat (180–230°C/350–450°).

4 Brush the cooking grates clean. Grill the lamb chops over medium grilling heat, with the lid closed as much as possible and turning once, until cooked to your desired doneness, about 10 minutes for medium rare. Remove from the grill and serve warm with the sauce.

King-Size
BEEF KEBABS
with SALSA VERDE

prep **20*** mins

bbq **7-8** mins

serves **4-6**

skill ★☆☆

*marinating: 1 hour

Special equipment: 12 bamboo skewers, soaked in water for at least 30 minutes

SAUCE

- 25 g (1 oz) flat leaf parsley, leaves and tender stems
- 1 tablespoon capers, rinsed and drained
- 2 anchovy fillets, coarsely chopped
- 2 hard-boiled egg yolks
- 75 ml (3 fl oz) extra-virgin olive oil
- 2 teaspoons red wine vinegar
- ¼ teaspoon sea salt
- ¼ teaspoon freshly ground black pepper

- 1 kg (2 lb) sirloin steak, about 3.5 cm (1½ inches) thick
- ½ teaspoon freshly ground black pepper
- ½ teaspoon garlic granules
- 2 tablespoons extra-virgin olive oil
- ½ teaspoon sea salt
- 12 slices ripe tomato (optional)

1 Finely chop the parsley, capers, anchovy fillets and egg yolks in a food processor. With the machine running add the oil in a steady stream, then add the vinegar, salt and pepper. The sauce can be made up to one day in advance and kept, covered, in the refrigerator. Stir sauce just before serving.

2 Trim the meat of any excess fat and cut into 3.5-cm (1½-inch) cubes. Season with the pepper and garlic granules, pressing the spices into the meat. Place the meat in a medium bowl, cover with clingfilm and refrigerate for about 1 hour.

3 Allow the meat to stand at room temperature for 20–30 minutes before grilling. Add the oil to the bowl, toss to coat the meat evenly and then thread the meat on to skewers. Sprinkle with the salt.

4 Prepare the grill for grilling over high heat (230–290°C/450–550°F).

5 Brush the cooking grates clean. Grill the kebabs on all four sides over high grilling heat, with the lid closed as much as possible and turning four times, until cooked to your desired doneness, 7–8 minutes for medium rare. Serve warm with the sauce on the side and with sliced tomatoes, if liked.

with Aubergine Caponata

prep 40 mins · bbq 16–22 mins · serves 4–6 · skill ★☆☆

CAPONATA

- 1 aubergine, ends trimmed and cut crossways into 1-cm (½-inch) slices
- 1 small onion, cut crossways into 1-cm (½-inch) slices
- Extra-virgin olive oil
- 1 large ripe tomato, cored and cut into 1-cm (½-inch) dice
- 16 kalamata olives, pitted and cut in half
- 2 tablespoons finely chopped fresh basil
- 1 tablespoon capers, drained
- 2 teaspoons balsamic vinegar
- 2 teaspoons finely chopped garlic
- Sea salt
- Freshly ground black pepper

- 4 T-bone steaks, each about 500 g (1 lb) and 2.5 cm (1 inch) thick
- 4 teaspoons herbes de Provence

1 Prepare the grill for grilling over medium heat (180–230°C/350–450°F).

2 Brush the aubergine and onion slices with oil. Brush the cooking grates clean. Grill over medium grilling heat for 8–12 minutes, with the lid closed as much as possible, until well marked and tender. Transfer to a chopping board and, when cool enough to handle, cut into 1-cm (½-inch) dice. Put the aubergine, onion and tomato in a medium bowl. Add the remaining caponata ingredients, including 2 tablespoons olive oil and salt and pepper to taste. Mix well. The caponata is best made a few hours before serving and left at room temperature.

3 Allow the steaks to stand at room temperature for 20–30 minutes before grilling. Increase the temperature of the grill to high heat (230–290°C/450–550°F). Lightly brush both sides of the steaks with oil and season evenly with the herbes de Provence, salt and pepper. Grill over high grilling heat, with the lid closed as much as possible and turning once or twice, until cooked to your desired doneness, 8–10 minutes for medium rare (if flare-ups occur, move the steaks temporarily over indirect heat). Transfer to a carving board and let rest for 3–5 minutes. Slice and serve warm with the caponata.

with Pizzaiola Sauce

 prep **15** mins

 bbq **15–21** mins

 serves **4**

 skill ★☆☆

SAUCE

- 1 kg (2 lb) plum tomatoes
- 2 tablespoons extra-virgin olive oil
- 1 tablespoon thinly sliced garlic
- 15 g (½ oz) thinly sliced oil-packed sun-dried tomatoes
- ¼ teaspoon crushed red chilli flakes
- Sea salt
- Freshly ground black pepper
- 2 tablespoons finely chopped oregano

- 750 g–1 kg (1½–2 lb) sirloin steak, about 3.5 cm (1½ inches) thick
- Extra-virgin olive oil

1 Prepare the grill for grilling and roasting over high heat (230–290°C/450–550°F).

2 Brush the cooking grates clean. Grill the tomatoes over high grilling heat for 3–5 minutes, with the lid closed as much as possible, until lightly charred on both sides. When cool enough to handle, peel away the skin, halve the tomatoes crossways, remove the cores, squeeze out the seeds, then roughly chop.

3 Warm the oil in a medium saucepan over medium heat and cook the garlic for 1–2 minutes until golden brown, stirring occasionally. Add the tomatoes, sun-dried tomatoes and chilli flakes. Reduce the heat and simmer for 15–20 minutes. Season with salt and pepper, then stir in the oregano.

4 Allow the steak to stand at room temperature for 20–30 minutes before grilling. Brush both sides of the steak with oil and season evenly with salt and pepper, rubbing the seasonings into the meat. Sear over high grilling heat for 8–10 minutes, with the lid closed as much as possible and turning once, and then finish grilling over high grilling heat until cooked to your desired doneness, 4–6 minutes for medium rare. Remove from the grill and let rest for 3–5 minutes. Reheat the sauce over a medium heat. Cut the steak into thick slices and serve over a pool of the sauce.

Spinach-Stuffed
BEEF FILLET
with HORSERADISH SAUCE

prep **30** mins

bbq **35–45** mins

serves **6–8**

skill ★★★

Special equipment: kitchen string

SAUCE

- 125 g (4 oz) soured cream
- 75 g (3 oz) mayonnaise
- 3 tablespoons prepared horseradish
- 15 g (½ oz) dill, finely chopped
- 1 tablespoon fresh lemon juice
- 1 teaspoon finely chopped garlic
- ¼ teaspoon sea salt
- ¼ teaspoon freshly ground black pepper

- 6 bacon rashers
- 1 tablespoon finely chopped garlic
- 250 g (8 oz) baby spinach
- 25 g (1 oz) raisins
- Freshly ground black pepper
- 1.5–1.75 kg (3–3-½ lb) whole beef fillet
- 15 g (½ oz) dill, finely chopped
- Sea salt

1 Whisk the sauce ingredients in a medium bowl. Cover and refrigerate until about 20 minutes before serving.

2 Cook the bacon in a large frying pan for about 10 minutes over a medium heat, turning occasionally, until crisp. Drain the bacon on kitchen paper. Pour off (and reserve) all but 2 tablespoons of the bacon fat in the pan. Add the garlic to the pan; cook for about 30 seconds, stirring occasionally. Add the spinach; cook for 1–2 minutes, stirring constantly, until the spinach is wilted. Place the spinach mixture in a medium bowl. Add the raisins and ⅛ teaspoon of pepper. Finely chop the bacon and add it to the bowl. Stir the mixture and allow it to cool to room temperature.

3 Trim the beef fillet of any excess fat and skin and allow to stand at room temperature for 20–30 minutes before grilling.

4 Prepare the grill for grilling and roasting over medium heat (180–230°C/350–450°F).

5 Using a long, narrow knife, make a hole through the centre along the full length of the fillet. Turn the knife over and cut to expand the opening. Stuff the spinach mixture into the hole from both ends using the handle of a spatula or a wooden spoon. Tie the beef with kitchen string into a compact, even cylinder. Lightly brush all over with some of the reserved bacon fat or with olive oil. Season with the dill, salt and pepper.

6 Brush the cooking grates clean. Sear the meat over medium grilling heat for 15 minutes, with the lid closed as much as possible, turning a quarter turn once every 3–4 minutes. Continue to roast over medium roasting heat, with the lid closed and turning once, until cooked to desired doneness, 20–30 minutes longer for medium rare. Remove from the grill and let rest for 5–10 minutes. Carefully cut into 1-cm (1-inch) slices. Serve warm with the sauce.

FILLET STEAK
with LEMON-PARSLEY BUTTER

prep 10 mins | bbq 8–10 mins | serves 4 | skill ★☆☆

BUTTER

- 50 g (2 oz) unsalted butter, softened
- 1 tablespoon finely chopped flat leaf parsley
- ¼ teaspoon grated lemon zest
- 1 teaspoon fresh lemon juice
- ¼ teaspoon sea salt
- ¼ teaspoon freshly ground black pepper

- 4 fillet steaks, each about 250 g (8 oz) and 3 cm (1¼ inches) thick
- Extra-virgin olive oil
- ½ teaspoon sea salt
- ½ teaspoon freshly ground black pepper

1 Combine the butter ingredients in a small bowl. Using the back of a fork, mash and stir until evenly distributed. Cover and refrigerate until ready to serve.

2 Lightly brush both sides of the steaks with oil and season evenly with the salt and pepper. Allow the steaks to stand at room temperature for 20–30 minutes before grilling.

3 Prepare the grill for grilling over high heat (230–290°C/450–550°F).

4 Brush the cooking grates clean. Grill the steaks over high grilling heat, with the lid closed as much as possible and turning once, until cooked to your desired doneness, 8–10 minutes for medium rare. Transfer each steak to a serving plate and place a tablespoon of the butter on top to melt. Serve warm.

Argentine
BEEF FILLET

SANDWICHES with Roasted Peppers and Sweet Onions

prep 30 mins

bbq 50–60 mins

serves 8

skill ★★☆

- 4 red peppers
- 2 teaspoons finely chopped garlic
- 2 onions, cut into 1-cm (½-inch) slices
- Extra-virgin olive oil
- 1.25 kg (2 lb 8 oz) whole beef fillet
- 1 teaspoon sea salt
- 2 teaspoons freshly ground black pepper
- 8 mini baguettes, split open
- 4 hard-boiled eggs, sliced crossways
- 8 large lettuce leaves
- 250 g (8 oz) good-quality mayonnaise

1 Prepare the grill for grilling and roasting over medium heat (180–230°C/350–450°F).

2 Brush the cooking grates clean. Grill the peppers over medium grilling heat for 12–15 minutes, with the lid closed as much as possible and turning occasionally, until the skins are blackened and blistered all over. Place the peppers in a small bowl and cover with clingfilm to trap the steam. Set aside for at least 10 minutes, then remove the peppers from the bowl and peel away the charred skins. Cut off the tops, remove the seeds and cut lengthways into 1-cm (½-inch) wide strips. Mix the peppers with the garlic in a large bowl.

3 Lightly brush or spray the onion slices with oil. Grill over medium grilling heat for 8–10 minutes, turning once, until nicely marked and tender. Cut the onion slices in half and add to the bowl with the peppers and garlic.

4 Trim the beef fillet of any excess fat and skin and allow to stand at room temperature for 20–30 minutes before grilling. Lightly brush with oil and rub the salt and pepper into the meat. Sear over medium grilling heat for about 15 minutes, with the lid closed as much as possible, turning a quarter turn every 3–4 minutes, until well marked. Move the meat over medium roasting heat and roast, with the lid closed as much as possible and turning once, until cooked to your desired doneness, 15–20 minutes for medium rare. Remove from the grill and let rest for 5–10 minutes. Cut into thin slices and place on a warm platter.

5 Grill the rolls, cut sides down, over medium grilling heat for about 30 seconds until lightly toasted. Allow guests to assemble sandwiches with beef, peppers, onions, eggs, lettuce and mayonnaise.

WHISKY
and Onion-Marinated
BRISKET

prep **20*** mins

bbq **4** hours

serves **4–6**

skill ★★☆

*marinating: 4 hours

Special equipment: large disposable aluminium foil roasting tray

RUB

- 1 tablespoon onion flakes
- 2 teaspoons celery salt
- 1 teaspoon dried dill
- ½ teaspoon sea salt
- ½ teaspoon freshly ground black pepper

- About 1.5 kg (3 lb) beef brisket, trimmed of surface fat
- Extra-virgin olive oil
- 125 ml (4 fl oz) whisky
- 475 ml (16 fl oz) beef or vegetable stock
- 750 g (1 lb 8 oz) small waxy potatoes
- 1 teaspoon sea salt
- ½ teaspoon finely ground fresh black pepper
- 300 g (10 oz) pickling onions, peeled
- 500 g (1 lb) baby carrots, peeled

1 Mix the rub ingredients in a small bowl. Press the rub into the meat and place in a large disposable foil roasting tray. Cover with clingfilm and refrigerate for 4 hours.

2 Remove the meat from the refrigerator and allow to stand at room temperature for about 30 minutes before grilling. Generously brush the brisket with olive oil.

3 Prepare the grill for grilling over high heat (230–290°C/450–550°F) and roasting over low heat (130–180°C/250–350°F).

4 Brush the cooking grates clean. Sear the brisket over high grilling heat for about 8 minutes, with the lid closed as much as possible and turning once, until browned. Transfer the meat to the foil tray. Pour in the whisky and stock, and cover the pan with aluminium foil.

5 Decrease the temperature of the grill to low heat. Roast the brisket in the roasting tray over low roasting heat for 2 hours with the lid closed, keeping the grill temperature about 150°C/300°F.

6 Cut the small potatoes in half (if the potatoes are larger than 6 cm/2½ inches in diameter, cut them into quarters). Combine the potatoes, ½ teaspoon of the salt and ¼ teaspoon of the pepper in a medium bowl. In another medium bowl combine the onions, carrots and the remaining salt and pepper.

7 After the 2 hours of roasting, uncover the meat, turn it over, place the potatoes around the edges and the onions and carrots on top. Cover the meat again and continue to cook for 2 hours more, or longer if not fork tender.

8 Remove the brisket and vegetables from the grill. Place the brisket on a carving board and cut across the grain into thin, diagonal slices. If liked, skim fat from the pan juices. Place on a serving platter, top with pan juices and surround with the vegetables.

Mount Olympus
MEATBALL
KEBABS

 prep **15*** mins

 bbq **8–10** mins

 serves **4–6**

skill ★☆☆

*marinating: 2–8 hours

Special equipment: 6 long, wide bamboo skewers, soaked in water for at least 30 minutes

MEATBALLS

- 2 garlic cloves
- 1 small red onion, roughly chopped
- 25 g (1 oz) mint leaves
- 375 g (12 oz) minced lamb
- 375 g (12 oz) minced beef
- 1 tablespoon red wine vinegar
- 1½ teaspoons sea salt
- 1 teaspoon freshly ground black pepper
- 1 teaspoon dried oregano
- ½ teaspoon paprika

SAUCE

- 125 g (4 oz) cucumber
- 250 g (8 oz) plain yogurt
- 2 tablespoons extra-virgin olive oil
- 15 g (½ oz) dill, finely chopped
- ½ teaspoon sea salt
- ¼ teaspoon freshly ground black pepper
- ⅛ teaspoon Tabasco sauce

- Extra-virgin olive oil

1 Finely chop the garlic, onion and mint in a food processor. In a medium bowl combine the contents of the food processor with the remaining meatball ingredients. Blend and squeeze the mixture with your hands until it is well combined. Lightly wet your hands with cold water, then shape the mixture into meatballs about 3.5 cm (1½ inches) in diameter (you should have about 20–25 meatballs). Thread long, wide skewers through the centre of the meatballs, four to five meatballs per skewer, leaving a little room between each meatball. Place the kebabs on a roasting tray, cover and refrigerate for 2 hours, or as long as 8 hours.

2 Grate the cucumber. Drain in a colander and squeeze out most of the moisture. In a medium bowl whisk the cucumber with the remaining sauce ingredients. Cover and refrigerate until ready to serve.

3 Prepare the grill for grilling over medium heat (180–230°C/350–450°F).

4 Lightly brush or spray the kebabs on all sides with oil. Brush the cooking grates clean. Grill the kebabs over medium grilling heat for 8–10 minutes, with the lid closed as much as possible and gently rotating the meatballs two or three times during grilling, until fully cooked. Serve warm with the sauce.

PORK

Citrus-Glazed
PORK
FILLET

prep **10*** mins   bbq **20–30** mins   serves **4**   skill ★☆☆

*marinating: 3–8 hours

MARINADE

- 2 tablespoons tomato ketchup
- 2 tablespoons hoisin sauce
- 1 tablespoon rice wine vinegar
- 2 teaspoons grated orange zest
- 1 teaspoon hot chilli sauce
- 1 teaspoon sesame oil
- ½ tablespoon soy sauce
- 1½ teaspoons curry powder

- 2 pork fillets, each 375–500 g (12 oz–1 lb)

1 Whisk the marinade ingredients in a medium bowl. Add the pork to the bowl and turn to coat well. Cover and refrigerate for 3 hours or as long as 8 hours. Allow the meat to stand at room temperature for 15–30 minutes before grilling.

2 Prepare the grill for roasting over medium heat (180–230°C/350–450°F).

3 Remove the pork from the marinade, wiping off most of the marinade. Brush the cooking grates clean. Roast over medium roasting heat for 20–30 minutes, with the lid closed as much as possible and turning once, until the centres are barely pink (the internal temperature should be 68–70°C/155–160°F). Remove the meat from the grill and let rest for 3–5 minutes. Cut into thick slices and serve warm.

FILLET

and BACON
with Stewed White Beans

prep **30** mins — bbq **20** mins — serves **4–6** — skill ★★★

- 2 teaspoons fennel seeds
- ½ teaspoon sea salt
- ½ teaspoon freshly ground black pepper
- 2 pork fillets, about 500 g (1 lb) each
- 12 thinly sliced bacon rashers, about 375 g (12 oz) total weight

BEANS

- 4 ripe plum tomatoes, about 500 g (1 lb) total weight, cored
- 2 tablespoons extra-virgin olive oil
- 1 onion, finely diced
- 1 tablespoon finely chopped garlic
- ¼ teaspoon crushed red chilli flakes (optional)
- 2 x 425-g (15-oz) cans cannellini beans, rinsed

- 25 g (1 oz) basil leaves, torn

1 Toast the fennel seeds in a small frying pan over a low heat for 3–5 minutes until the aroma is apparent, shaking the pan occasionally. Crush the fennel seeds in a spice grinder or on a chopping board by grinding them under a heavy pan. Combine in a small bowl with the salt and pepper.

2 Trim any excess fat and skin from the pork fillets. Cut into pieces about 3.5 cm (1½ inches) long. Season them with the fennel mixture. Gently press down on each piece to form a disc the same thickness as the width of the bacon. Wrap a piece of bacon around each piece of pork and secure with a cocktail stick. The bacon should overlap at the ends by no more than 2.5 cm (1 inch). Allow to stand at room temperature for 10–15 minutes before grilling.

3 Prepare the grill for grilling over medium heat (180–230°C/350–450°F).

4 Brush the cooking grates clean. Grill the tomatoes over medium grilling heat for 6–8 minutes, with the lid closed as much as possible and turning occasionally, until the skins are loosened. Cut the tomatoes into 2.5-cm (1-inch) chunks.

5 Warm the oil in a medium saucepan over a medium heat, then cook the onion, garlic and chilli flakes for about 3 minutes, stirring occasionally, until softened. Add the tomatoes and beans, stir to combine, and season with salt and pepper. When the beans come to the boil, reduce the heat and simmer for 15 minutes.

6 Grill the pork over medium grilling heat for 12–15 minutes, with the lid closed as much as possible and turning once, until barely pink in the centre and the bacon is fully cooked. Remove from the grill and let rest for 3–5 minutes. Add the basil to the beans. Serve the pork warm with the beans.

West Indies
PORK CHOPS
with Black Bean-Mango Salsa

prep **15*** mins

bbq **6–8** mins

serves **4**

skill ★☆☆

*marinating: 1–2 hours

SALSA

- 250 g (8 oz) canned black beans, rinsed
- 1 large mango, about 500 g (1 lb), cut into 5-mm (¼-inch) dice
- 4 spring onions (white and light green parts only), thinly sliced
- 20 g (¾ oz) basil, finely chopped
- 1 tablespoon extra-virgin olive oil
- 2 teaspoons fresh lime juice
- ¼ teaspoon sea salt
- ⅛ teaspoon freshly ground black pepper
- ⅛ teaspoon ground cumin
- ⅛ teaspoon chilli powder

RUB

- 1 teaspoon light brown sugar
- 1 teaspoon garlic granules
- 1 teaspoon dried thyme
- ¾ teaspoon sea salt
- ¼ teaspoon freshly ground black pepper
- ¼ teaspoon ground allspice

- 4 pork chops, each about 250 g (8 oz) and 1.5 cm (¾ inch) thick
- Extra-virgin olive oil

1 Mix the salsa ingredients in a medium bowl. To fully incorporate the flavours, let the salsa sit at room temperature for 1–2 hours.

2 Mix the rub ingredients with your fingertips in a small bowl. Lightly brush the chops on both sides with oil and season with the rub. Allow the chops to stand at room temperature for 20–30 minutes before grilling.

3 Prepare the grill for grilling over high heat (230–290°C/450–550°F).

4 Brush the cooking grates clean. Grill the chops over high grilling heat for 6–8 minutes, with the lid closed as much as possible and turning once or twice, until barely pink in the centre of the meat. Remove from the grill and let rest for 3–5 minutes. Serve warm with the salsa.

PORK CHOPS

prep **10*** mins

bbq **8–10** mins

serves **6**

skill ★★☆

*marinating: 2–4 hours

MARINADE

- 4 tablespoons tomato ketchup
- 2 tablespoons apple juice
- 2 tablespoons extra-virgin olive oil
- 2 tablespoons red wine vinegar
- 1 tablespoon Worcestershire sauce
- 2 teaspcons finely chopped garlic
- 1 teaspcon Tabasco sauce
- 1 teaspcon chilli powder
- ½ teaspoon sea salt

- 6 pork chops, each about 1 cm (1 inch) thick

1 Whisk all the marinade ingredients together in a medium bowl.

2 Place the chops in a large, resealable plastic bag and pour in the marinade. Press the air out of the bag and seal it tightly. Turn the bag several times to distribute the marinade, and refrigerate for 2–4 hours.

3 Remove the chops from the bag and discard the marinade. Allow the chops to stand at room temperature for 20–30 minutes before grilling.

4 Prepare the grill for grilling over medium heat (180–230°C/350–450°F).

5 Brush the cooking grates clean. Grill the chops over medium grilling heat for 8–10 minutes, with the lid closed as much as possible and turning once, until barely pink in the centre of the meat. Let rest for 3–5 minutes. Serve warm.

ROTISSERIE PORK
with Whisky Barbecue Mop

prep **30*** mins

bbq **3½–4** hours

serves **12**

skill ★★★

*marinating: 12–24 hours

Special equipment: spice mill, rotisserie, kitchen string

RUB

- 2 teaspoons whole black peppercorns
- 2 teaspoons mustard seed
- 1½ tablespoons light brown sugar
- 1 teaspoon garlic granules
- 1 teaspoon onion flakes
- 1 teaspoon paprika

- 2.5–3 kg (5–6 lb) boneless pork shoulder, rolled and tied
- 1 tablespoon sea salt

MOP

- 250 ml (8 fl oz) whisky
- 1 small onion, about 150 g (5 oz), puréed
- 90 g (3½ oz) light brown sugar
- 4 tablespoons golden syrup
- 4 tablespoons tomato ketchup
- 25 g (1 oz) coarse brown or wholegrain mustard

1 Pulverize the peppercorns with the mustard seeds in a spice mill. Pour into a small bowl and combine with the remaining rub ingredients.

2 Season the pork with the rub. Wrap in clingfilm and place on a plate. Refrigerate for 12–24 hours. Allow the pork to stand at room temperature for 45 minutes before grilling. Season with the salt.

3 Meanwhile, make the mop. Whisk the mop ingredients together in a medium bowl.

4 Follow the grill's instructions for using the rotisserie and prepare the grill for grilling over low heat (130–180°C/250–350°F). Centre the pork on the spit and secure it in place. Rotate over low grilling heat for 3½–4 hours, or 30 minutes per 500 g (1 lb), with the lid closed as much as possible, until the internal temperature reaches 80°C (175°F.) After the first hour, if the pork starts looking too brown, finish grilling over low grilling heat. After the first hour, baste the pork generously with the mop every 20 minutes. Remove from the rotisserie, loosely cover with foil, and let rest for about 20 minutes before slicing. Serve warm.

Mustard-Molasses
GLAZED HAM

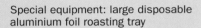

prep **10** mins — bbq **3–3½** hours — serves **10–12** — skill ★★☆

Special equipment: large disposable aluminium foil roasting tray

GLAZE
- 125 g (4 oz) wholegrain mustard
- 4 tablespoons black treacle
- 4 tablespoons fresh orange juice
- 1 teaspoon ground ginger
- ¼ teaspoon ground cloves

- About 5 kg (10 lb) smoked gammon joint, bone-in

1 Combine the glaze ingredients in a small saucepan. Bring the glaze to a simmer over a medium-high heat, stirring occasionally. Simmer for 1 minute, then remove the pan from the heat.

2 Allow the gammon to stand at room temperature for about 30 minutes before grilling. Prepare the grill for roasting over medium heat (180–230°C/350–450°F).

3 Score the meat by making cross-hatches about 2.5 cm (1 inch) apart and 1 cm (½ inch) deep over the entire surface, except on the flat side. Place the gammon, flat side down, in a disposable foil roasting tray. Brush the cooking grates clean. Roast over medium roasting heat for 1 hour with the lid closed. Brush the glaze over the entire surface of the ham, except on the flat side. Continue to roast for a further 2–2½ hours, until the internal temperature reaches 70°C/160°F.

4 Transfer the gammon to a carving board and loosely cover with foil. Let rest for about 15 minutes. Slice and serve warm or at room temperature.

Beer-Bathed German
SAUSAGE
with Sauerkraut and Apples

prep
10
mins

bbq
25
mins

serves
5

skill
★☆☆

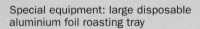

Special equipment: large disposable aluminium foil roasting tray

- 5 fresh bratwurst sausages
- 1 small onion
- 1 small Granny Smith apple
- 250 g (8 oz) sauerkraut, rinsed and drained
- 350 ml (12 fl oz) beer, at room temperature
- 3 tablespoons spicy German mustard
- 1 teaspoon caraway seeds (optional)
- 5 hot dog buns

1 Prepare the grill for grilling over medium heat (180–230°C/350–450°F).

2 Arrange the sausages in a single layer in a large disposable foil roasting tray. Peel the onion and trim off the ends. Cut in half lengthways, then cut each half lengthways into 2.5-mm (⅛-inch) slices. Core and quarter the apple, and cut lengthways into 2.5-mm (⅛-inch) slices. Scatter the onion, apple and sauerkraut over the sausages.

3 Mix the beer, mustard and caraway seeds, if using, in a medium bowl. Add the beer mixture to the roasting tray. Brush the cooking grates clean. Grill over medium grilling heat for about 20 minutes, with the lid closed as much as possible and turning the sausages two or three times. Remove the sausages from the tray but leave the tray where it is to continue to cook the sauerkraut mixture. Grill the sausages over medium grilling heat for 2–3 minutes, turning once, until nicely browned. Serve the sausages warm in hot dog buns with the sauerkraut mixture. Serve more mustard on top, if liked.

Everybody's Favourite
DRY RIBS

prep **15** mins

bbq **1½–2** hours

serves **6**

skill ★★☆

Special equipment: spice mill

RUB
- 40 g (1½ oz) sea salt
- 40 g (1½ oz) whole black peppercorns
- 25 g (1 oz) granulated sugar
- 1½ tablespoons mustard seeds
- 1½ tablespoons sweet paprika
- 2 teaspoons dried oregano
- 1½ teaspoons cumin seeds
- 1½ teaspoons fennel seeds
- 1½ teaspoons celery seed
- 1½ teaspoons crushed red chilli flakes
- 1 teaspoon dried thyme

- 2–3 slabs meaty pork spareribs, 3–3.5 kg (6–7 lb) total weight, trimmed of excess fat

- Hickory chunks or chips, soaked in water for at least 30 minutes

1 Pulse the rub ingredients for a few seconds in a spice mill (in two batches, if necessary) until the seeds are coarsely ground. The rub should have a slightly coarse texture. Spread the rub generously on all sides of the ribs and allow to stand at room temperature for 20–30 minutes before grilling.

2 Prepare the grill for roasting over medium heat (180–230°C/350–450°F).

3 Follow the grill's instructions for using wood chunks. Brush the cooking grates clean. Roast the ribs, bone side down, over medium roasting heat for 1½–2 hours, with the lid closed as much as possible, until the meat is very tender and has pulled back from the ends of the bones. Remove from the grill and allow to rest for 5–10 minutes before slicing into individual ribs.

PEPPERONI
Pizzas

prep
30
mins

bbq
6–8
mins

serves
4

skill
★★☆

DOUGH

- 1 sachet dry yeast
- ½ teaspoon granulated sugar
- 175 ml (6 fl oz) warm water (40–46°C/105–115°F)
- 375 g (12 oz) plain flour, plus more for rolling dough
- Extra-virgin olive oil
- 1 teaspoon sea salt

- 375 g (12 oz) low-fat mozzarella cheese, coarsely grated
- 250 g (8 oz) pepperoni sausage, cut into 5-mm (¼-inch) slices
- 1 roasted red pepper, thinly sliced
- 250 g (8 oz) good-quality tomato sauce
- 1 teaspoon dried oregano

1 Combine the yeast and sugar with the water in a medium bowl. Stir once and let stand for 5–10 minutes until foamy. Add the flour, 3 tablespoons of olive oil and the salt. Stir until the dough holds together. Transfer to a lightly floured work surface and knead for 4–6 minutes until smooth. Shape into a ball and place in a lightly oiled bowl. Turn the ball to cover the surface with oil. Cover the bowl with kitchen paper and set aside in a warm place for 1–1½ hours until the dough doubles in size.

2 Prepare the grill for baking over medium heat (180–230°C/350–450°F).

3 Punch down the dough in the bowl. Transfer to a lightly floured surface and cut into four equal pieces. Cut baking paper into 23-cm (9-inch) squares and lightly oil each sheet of paper on one side. Press the dough flat on the oiled side of the paper into circles about 20 cm (8 inches) in diameter. Lightly oil the top side of the dough.

4 Brush the cooking grates clean. Lay the dough on the grate, with the paper side facing up. Grab one corner of the paper with tongs and peel it off. Bake the dough over medium baking heat for 2–3 minutes, with the lid closed as much as possible and rotating the pizza bases occasionally for even cooking, until they are marked on the underside. Transfer the bases from the cooking grate to the back of a baking sheet, with the grilled sides facing up.

5 Arrange a quarter of the cheese on each base, leaving a 1-cm (½-inch) border around the edges. Arrange the pepperoni and red peppers over the cheese. Spoon the

tomato sauce here and there, being careful not to wet the dough with too much watery sauce. Sprinkle the oregano over the pizzas. Transfer the pizzas from the baking sheet to the grate. Bake for 4–5 minutes, rotating the pizzas occasionally, until the crusts are crisp and the cheese is melted. Transfer to a chopping board. Cut into wedges. Serve warm.

Greek
CHICKEN SALAD
SANDWICHES

prep	bbq	serves	skill
15* mins	8–10 mins	4	★☆☆

*marinating time: 2–3 hours

MARINADE

- Zest and juice of 1 lemon
- 2 tablespoons extra-virgin olive oil
- 15 g (½ oz) oregano, finely chopped
- 15 g (½ oz) dill, finely chopped
- ½ teaspoon garlic granules
- ¼ teaspoon mustard powder
- ¼ teaspoon ground cumin
- ¼ teaspoon ground coriander
- ¼ teaspoon sea salt
- ¼ teaspoon ground cayenne pepper

- 8 boneless, skinless chicken thighs, each about 125 g (4 oz)

- 175 ml (6 fl oz) creamy cucumber or blue cheese dressing

- 4 pitta breads
- 8 small green lettuce leaves
- 8 thin slices ripe tomato

1 Whisk the marinade ingredients together in a small bowl.

2 Place the chicken thighs in a large, resealable plastic bag and pour in the marinade. Press the air out of the bag and seal tightly. Turn the bag several times to distribute the marinade. Refrigerate for 2–3 hours.

3 Prepare the grill for grilling over high heat (230–290°C/450–550°F).

4 Remove the chicken from the bag and discard the marinade. Brush the cooking grates clean. Grill the thighs over high grilling heat for 8–10 minutes, with the lid closed as much as possible and turning once or twice, until the meat is firm and the juices run clear. Remove from the grill and let rest for a few minutes until cool enough to handle. Chop into 5-mm (¼-inch) pieces and place in a bowl. Add enough of the dressing to coat the thigh pieces. Mix well.

5 Cut each pitta bread into two half-moons. Open the 8 halves and slide a lettuce leaf and tomato slice into each one. Fill with the chicken salad. Serve at room temperature.

Citrus-Avocado
CHICKEN
BREASTS

prep
- 40* -
mins

bbq
- 8–12 -
mins

serves
4

skill
★☆☆

* **marinating: 4–8 hours**

SALSA
- 2 limes
- 2 oranges
- 1 grapefruit
- 25 g (1 oz) redcurrants
- 1 serrano chilli, deseeded and finely chopped
- 1 spring onion (white part only), finely chopped
- 1 tablespoon finely chopped basil
- 1 tablespoon finely chopped fresh coriander
- 1 tablespoon honey
- 1 teaspoon finely chopped Anaheim chilli

MARINADE
- 25 g (1 oz) citrus zest, reserved from the salsa
- 125 ml (4 fl oz) citrus juice, reserved from the salsa
- 2 tablespoons honey
- 1 tablespoon extra-virgin olive oil
- 1 teaspoon finely chopped garlic
- 1 serrano chilli, deseeded and finely chopped
- 1 tablespoon finely chopped basil
- 1 tablespoon finely chopped fresh coriander
- ½ teaspoon ground cumin

- 4 boneless, skinless chicken breasts, each about 175 g (6 oz)

- 2 firm, ripe avocados
- Sea salt

- Extra-virgin olive oil

1 Wash and dry the limes, oranges and grapefruit. Grate their zests and set the zest aside for use in the marinade. With a sharp paring knife, peel and section the citrus fruit, reserving the membranes. Squeeze the juice from the membranes (you should have about 125 ml/4 fl oz) and reserve the juice for the marinade. Discard the membranes. Cut each citrus segment into three or four pieces and place in a large stainless-steel mixing bowl with the remaining salsa ingredients. Mix thoroughly, cover and refrigerate until 1 hour before serving.

2 Whisk the reserved citrus zests and juices with the remaining marinade ingredients in a small bowl.

3 Place the chicken breasts in a large, resealable plastic bag and pour in the marinade. Press the air out of the bag and seal tightly. Turn the bag to distribute the marinade, place in a bowl and refrigerate for 4–8 hours, turning occasionally.

4 Cut the avocados in half and remove the stones. Peel and discard the skin and cut the avocado into chunks. Lightly mix into the salsa and season with salt. Let the salsa stand at room temperature for up to 1 hour to blend the flavours fully.

5 Prepare the grill for grilling over medium heat (180–230°C/350–450°F).

6 Remove the chicken breasts from the bag and discard the marinade. Lightly brush on both sides with olive oil and season with salt. Brush the cooking grates clean. Grill the chicken breasts over medium grilling heat for 8–12 minutes, with the lid closed as much as possible and turning once, until the juices run clear and the meat is no longer pink in the centre. Remove from the grill and serve warm with the salsa.

CHICKEN
Under BRICKS

prep **35*** mins

bbq **32–43** mins

serves **8**

skill ★★★

*marinating: 8–24 hours

Special equipment: 3 bricks, wrapped in foil

PASTE

- 1 whole head garlic, cloves finely chopped
- 30 g (1 oz) wholegrain mustard
- 15 g (½ oz) thyme, finely chopped
- 15 g (½ oz) rosemary, finely chopped
- 30 g (1 oz) coarsely ground white pepper
- 2 tablespoons fresh lemon juice
- 2 tablespoons extra-virgin olive oil

- 2 chickens, each about 2 kg (4 lb)
- Extra-virgin olive oil
- Sea salt

1 Mix the paste ingredients in a small bowl.

2 Remove and discard the neck, giblets and any excess fat from the chickens. Remove the backbones and cut in half. Coat each chicken half thoroughly with the paste. Place the chicken halves in a large, resealable plastic bag (if one bag isn't large enough, use two). Press the air out of the bag, seal tightly, and refrigerate for 8–24 hours.

3 Prepare the grill for roasting over high heat (230–290°C/450–550°F).

4 Lightly brush the chicken halves with olive oil. Season with salt. Brush the cooking grates clean. Place the chickens, skin side down, over high roasting heat. Lightly coat the bottom of a roasting tray with oil. Wrap three bricks in aluminium foil. Place the roasting tray on top of the chicken halves and weight the tray down with 3 bricks wrapped in foil. Roast the chickens for 30–40 minutes, with the lid closed, until the skin is crispy and the juices run clear. Wearing insulated barbecue mitts or oven gloves, carefully remove the bricks and tray. Turn the chickens and continue to roast for 2–3 minutes to crisp the underside. Transfer from the grill to a platter, loosely cover with foil and allow to rest for about 5 minutes before cutting the halves in two. Serve warm.

Mojo-Marinated
CHICKEN

prep **10*** mins — bbq **30–40** mins — serves **4** — skill ★☆☆

*marinating: 6–8 hours

MARINADE

- 125 ml (4 fl oz) fresh orange juice
- 2 tablespoons fresh lime juice
- 2 tablespoons soy sauce
- 2 tablespoons extra-virgin olive oil
- 1 tablespoon finely chopped garlic
- ½ teaspoon Tabasco sauce
- ½ teaspoon ground cumin
- ¼ teaspoon sea salt
- ¼ teaspoon freshly ground black pepper

- 4 chicken breasts (with bone and skin), each 300–375 g (10–12 oz)

1 Whisk all the marinade ingredients together in a medium bowl.

2 Place the chicken in a large, resealable plastic bag and pour in the marinade. Press the air out of the bag and seal tightly. Turn the bag to distribute the marinade, place in a bowl and refrigerate for 6–8 hours, turning occasionally.

3 Prepare the grill for roasting over medium heat (180–230°C/350–450°F).

4 Remove the chicken from the bag and reserve the marinade. Pour the marinade into a small saucepan, bring to the boil over a high heat and boil for 1 minute.

5 Brush the cooking grates clean. Roast the chicken, bone side down, over medium roasting heat for 30–40 minutes, with the lid closed as much as possible and basting once or twice with the boiled marinade, until the juices run clear and the meat is no longer pink at the bone. For crispier skin, grill the chicken, skin side down, over medium grilling heat during the last 5 minutes of cooking time. Brush with a little of the boiled marinade just before serving.

Chicken

prep
20*
mins

bbq
-30–50-
mins

serves
4

skill
★☆☆

*marinating: 6–12 hours

PASTE

- 4 spring onions (white part only), coarsely chopped
- 1 habanero chilli, deseeded and coarsely chopped
- 3 tablespoons rapeseed oil
- 2 tablespoons fresh lime juice
- 1 tablespoon garlic granules
- 2 teaspoons dried thyme
- 2 teaspoons ground allspice
- 1 teaspoon granulated sugar
- 1 teaspoon sea salt
- ½ teaspoon freshly ground black pepper

- 1.75–2 kg (3 lb 8 oz–4 lb) whole chicken, cut into 8 serving pieces

1 Combine the paste ingredients in a food processor and process until smooth. Rub the paste all over the chicken pieces, cover with clingfilm, and refrigerate the chicken for 6–12 hours.

2 Prepare the grill for roasting over medium heat (180–230°C/350–450°F).

3 Brush the cooking grates clean. Roast the chicken pieces, skin side up, over medium roasting heat, with the lid closed, until the juices run clear and the meat is opaque all the way to the bone. The leg and thigh pieces will take 40–50 minutes and the breast and wing pieces will take 30–40 minutes. For crispier skin, grill the chicken, skin side down, over medium grilling heat during the last 5–10 minutes of cooking time. Remove from the grill and serve warm.

CHICKEN
in Red Wine Marinade

 prep **20*** mins

 bbq **40–50** mins

 serves **4**

 skill ★★★

*marinating: 24 hours

MARINADE

- 1 large onion, quartered
- 6 large garlic cloves
- 50 g (2 oz) can anchovy fillets, drained
- Extra-virgin olive oil
- 50 g (2 oz) flat leaf parsley, leaves and tender stems
- 25 g (1 oz) rosemary leaves
- Sea salt
- Freshly ground black pepper
- 750 ml (1¼ pints) dry red wine

- 2 whole chickens, each about 1.5 kg (3 lb), excess fat removed

1 Combine the onion, garlic, anchovies, 125 ml (4 fl oz) olive oil, the parsley, rosemary, 1 teaspoon salt and 1 teaspoon pepper in a food processor. Process until the onion is finely chopped.

2 Place each chicken, breast side down, on a chopping board. Using poultry shears, cut along each side of the backbone and remove it. Open each chicken like a book. Split each chicken in half by cutting right along one side of the breastbone. Remove and discard the wing tips. Put the chicken halves in a large, resealable plastic bag (if one bag isn't large enough, use two). Pour the marinade into the bag and add the wine. Press the air out of the bag and seal tightly. Turn the bag to distribute the marinade, place in a bowl and refrigerate for 24 hours, turning occasionally (the meat and skin will be red in places from the wine).

3 Prepare the grill for roasting over medium heat (180–230°C/350–450°F).

4 Remove the chicken from the bag and discard the marinade. Pat dry with kitchen paper, brush all over with olive oil and season with ½ teaspoon salt and ¼ teaspoon pepper.

5 Brush the cooking grates clean. Roast the chicken, skin side up, over medium roasting heat for 40–50 minutes, with the lid closed. For crispier skin, turn and move over medium griling heat for the last 5–10 minutes (watch for flare-ups). Remove from the grill and let rest for about 5 minutes before cutting into pieces. Serve warm.

Bottle o' Beer
CHICKEN
THIGHS

prep
15*
mins

bbq
20
mins

serves
4

skill
★★☆

*marinating: 6–8 hours

MARINADE

- 350 ml (12 fl oz) beer, preferably lager
- 50 g (2 oz) Dijon mustard
- 3 tablespoons extra-virgin olive oil
- 6 spring onions (white and light green parts only), thinly sliced
- 2 large garlic cloves, thinly sliced
- 1 tablespoon Worcestershire sauce
- 1 teaspoon sea salt
- ½ teaspoon freshly ground black pepper
- ¼ teaspoon Tabasco sauce

- 8 chicken thighs (with bone and skin), each 150–170 g (5–6 oz)

1 Whisk the marinade ingredients in a medium bowl.

2 Trim the thighs of any excess skin and fat. Place in a large, resealable plastic bag and pour in the marinade. Press the air out of the bag and seal tightly. Turn the bag to distribute the marinade, place in a bowl and refrigerate for 6–8 hours, turning occasionally.

3 Prepare the grill for grilling over medium heat (180–230°C/350–450°F).

4 Remove the chicken from the bag and discard the marinade. Pat dry with kitchen paper. Brush the cooking grates clean. Grill the chicken thighs, skin side down first, over medium grilling heat for about 20 minutes, with the lid closed as much as possible and turning every 5 minutes, until the meat next to the bone is opaque. Serve warm.

Coriander-Pesto CHICKEN STRIPS

prep **10*** mins

bbq **6–8** mins

serves **4–6**

skill ★☆☆

*marinating: 2 hours

Special equipment: 12 bamboo skewers, soaked in water for at least 30 minutes

MARINADE

- 25 g (1 oz) walnuts, coarsely chopped
- 2 medium garlic cloves
- 175 g (6 oz) fresh coriander, leaves and tender stems
- 50 g (2 oz) flat leaf parsley, leaves and tender stems
- ½ teaspoon sea salt
- ¼ teaspoon freshly ground black pepper
- 2 tablespoons extra-virgin olive oil

- 1 kg (2 lb) chicken breast strips
- 1 lime, cut into wedges

1 Finely chop the walnuts and garlic in a food processor. Scrape down the side of the bowl. Add the coriander, parsley, salt and pepper and process until finely chopped. With the motor running, slowly add the oil to create a smooth purée.

2 Place the chicken in a large, resealable plastic bag and add the marinade. Press the air out of the bag and seal tightly. Turn the bag to distribute the marinade, place in a bowl and refrigerate for 2 hours.

3 Prepare the grill for grilling over high heat (230–290°C/450–550°F).

4 Remove the chicken from the bag and thread on to skewers. Brush the cooking grates clean. Grill over high grilling heat for 6–8 minutes, with the lid closed as much as possible and turning once, until the meat is firm and the juices run clear. Remove from the grill and serve warm with the lime wedges.

Risotto

prep **50*** mins · bbq **10–12** mins · serves **4** · skill ★★☆

*marinating: 2–6 hours

- 1 tablespoon brown sugar
- 1½ tablespoons sea salt
- ½ teaspoon freshly ground black pepper
- 2 boneless chicken breasts (with skin)

- Hickory wood chips, soaked in water for 30 minutes

- 150 g (5 oz) mangetout, trimmed
- 1–1.2 litres (1¾–2 pints) chicken stock
- 125 g (4 oz) unsalted butter
- 1 teaspoon finely chopped garlic
- 1 onion, finely diced
- 250 g (8 oz) Arborio rice
- 2 bay leaves
- 15 g (½ oz) flat leaf parsley, finely chopped
- 40 g (1½ oz) freshly grated Parmesan cheese

1 Mix the sugar, salt and pepper in a small bowl. Coat the chicken breasts evenly with the mixture, put them in a medium bowl, cover and refrigerate for at least 2 hours or as long as 6 hours.

2 Prepare the grill for grilling over medium heat (180–230°C/350–450°F).

3 Follow the grill's instructions for using wood chips. Brush the cooking grates clean. Grill the chicken, skin side down, over medium grilling heat for 10–12 minutes, with the lid closed as much as possible and turning once, until the meat is opaque throughout and the juices run clear. Remove from the grill and thinly slice the chicken.

4 Bring a medium saucepan filled three-quarters with salted water to the boil. Add the mangetout and parboil for about 3 minutes until barely tender. Drain and immediately cool under cold running water. Drain again and cut into 1-cm (½-inch) pieces.

5 Bring the chicken stock to a simmer in a medium saucepan. Melt half the butter in a large saucepan over a medium heat. Add the garlic and onion and cook for about 5 minutes, stirring occasionally, until soft. Add the rice and stir until the grains are coated with butter. Add about 125 ml (4 fl oz) of the simmering stock and the bay leaves and simmer, stirring continuously, until the rice absorbs almost all of the liquid. Add another 125 ml (4 fl oz) of the stock. Continue to stir until the rice absorbs the liquid. Continue adding stock and stirring until the rice is almost tender, about 25 minutes in total. Remove the bay leaves. Add the parsley, cheese and the remaining butter along with the chicken and mangetout. Stir and cook only enough to mix in the ingredients and warm them. Season with salt and pepper. Serve immediately.

Whole Roasted
TURKEY BREAST
with Sage and Parma Ham

 prep
20
mins

 bbq
-1–1¼-
hours

 serves
4

 skill
★★★

Special equipment: kitchen string

RUB

- 1 tablespoon finely chopped sage
- 2 teaspoons sea salt
- 1 teaspoon finely chopped garlic
- 1 teaspoon freshly grated lemon zest
- ¼ teaspoon freshly ground black pepper

- About 1 kg (2 lb 8 oz) whole boneless turkey breast (with skin)
- 6 thin slices Parma ham, about 75 g (3 oz) total weight
- 1 tablespoon extra-virgin olive oil

1 Mix the rub ingredients in a small bowl.

2 Gently slide your fingertips under the skin of the turkey breast on one side so that it pulls away from the meat, but leave the skin attached to the meat on all other sides. Spread some of the rub under the skin and pull the skin back in place. Coat the rest of the breast with the remaining rub, pressing it into the meat.

3 Arrange four to six 45-cm (18-inch) pieces of kitchen string on a work surface, each 7.5–10 cm (3–4 inches) apart and perpendicular to the edge of the work surface. Lay three of the ham slices vertically, side by side, over the string. Place the turkey breast, skin side down, on the ham and bring up the ends of the ham around the turkey breast. Place the remaining three Parma ham slices over the turkey breast to enclose the rest of the exposed meat. Tie the roast securely with the pieces of string. Rub the breast with the olive oil.

4 Prepare the grill for grilling and roasting over medium heat (180–230°C/350–450°F).

5 Brush the cooking grates clean. Sear the breast over medium grilling heat for 15 minutes, with the lid closed as much as possible and turning three times, until well marked on all sides. Move to medium roasting heat, close the lid and roast for 45–60 minutes, turning two or three times, until the internal temperature reaches 75°C (165°F). Remove from the grill and let rest for about 15 minutes before carving (the internal temperature will rise 5–10° during this time). Remove the string and slice into 5-mm (¼-inch) slices.

TURKEY BURGERS
with Creamy Cucumber
RELISH

prep
20
mins

bbq
5–7
mins

serves
4

skill
★★☆

BURGERS

- 625 g (1 lb 4 oz) minced turkey or chicken
- 50 g (2 oz) bread crumbs
- 4 spring onions (white and light green parts only), finely chopped
- 15 g (½ oz) basil, finely chopped
- 2 tablespoons fresh lime juice
- 1 tablespoon soy sauce
- 2 teaspoons finely chopped garlic
- ¼ teaspoon chilli powder
- ¼ teaspoon sea salt
- ¼ teaspoon freshly ground black pepper

RELISH

- 250 g (8 oz) cucumber, coarsely grated
- 25 g (1 oz) soured cream
- 1 tablespoon finely chopped dill
- 1 teaspoon finely chopped jalapeño chilli
- ½ teaspoon finely chopped garlic
- ¼ teaspoon sea salt
- ⅛ teaspoon freshly ground black pepper

- Extra-virgin olive oil

1 Mix the burger ingredients in a large bowl. Lightly wet your hands and shape the mixture into eight equal-sized balls. Place them on a baking sheet; press down gently to create burgers about 1.5 cm (¾ inch) thick. Cover with clingfilm and refrigerate until ready to grill.

2 Put the cucumber in a fine sieve and squeeze out the excess moisture. Mix the cucumber with the remaining relish ingredients in a medium bowl. Cover with clingfilm and refrigerate until ready to serve.

3 Prepare the grill for grilling over medium heat (180–230°C/350–450°F).

4 Generously brush the burgers on both sides with oil. Brush the cooking grates clean. Grill over medium grilling heat for 5–7 minutes, with the lid closed as much as possible and turning once, until just cooked through (cut one burger open to check). Serve burgers warm with the relish spooned over the top.

Crispy
DUCK BREASTS
with Orange-Ginger Glaze

prep
15*
mins

bbq
12–15
mins

serves
4

skill
★★☆

*marinating: 1–2 hours

MARINADE
- 4 tablespoons orange juice concentrate
- 4 tablespoons hoisin sauce
- 1 tablespoon cider vinegar
- 1 tablespoon grated ginger
- 2 teaspoons dark sesame oil
- 1 teaspoon finely chopped garlic
- ½ teaspoon sea salt
- ½ teaspoon freshly ground black pepper
- ¼ teaspoon Tabasco sauce

- 4 boneless duck breasts, each 175–250 g (6–8 oz) and about 1 cm (½ inch) thick
- Orange slices (optional)
- Pomegranate seeds (optional)

1 Whisk the marinade ingredients together in a large bowl.

2 Trim the duck breasts of any skin or fat that hangs over the edges. Score the skin in a diamond pattern with cross-hatches at 1 cm (½-inch) intervals, but do not cut into the flesh. Place the duck in a large, resealable plastic bag and pour in the marinade. Press the air out of the bag and seal tightly. Turn the bag to distribute the marinade, place in a bowl and refrigerate for 1–2 hours.

3 Prepare the grill for grilling over low heat (130–180°C/250–350°F).

4 Remove the duck from the bag and discard the marinade. Grill, skin side down first, over low grilling heat for 12–15 minutes, with the lid closed as much as possible and turning once, until the internal temperature reaches 70°C (160°F). The juices should be slightly pink, the skin, golden brown and crisp. Remove from the grill and let rest for 3–5 minutes. Garnish with orange slices and pomegranate seeds, if liked, and serve warm.

Spicy SEAFOOD
BOWL

prep
30
mins

bbq
4–6
mins

serves
4

skill
★★☆

SAUCE

- 1 tablespoon extra-virgin olive oil
- ½ onion, finely chopped
- 2 teaspoons finely chopped garlic
- ¼ teaspoon crushed red chilli flakes
- 450-g (14½-oz) can chopped tomatoes with juice
- 4 tablespoons dry white wine
- 1 tablespoon tomato purée
- 1 tablespoon finely chopped flat leaf parsley
- 1 teaspoon granulated sugar
- ½ teaspoon dried thyme
- ½ teaspoon dried oregano leaves
- ¼ teaspoon sea salt
- ¼ teaspoon freshly ground black pepper

- 8 small clams
- 8 large scallops, each about 40 g (1½ oz)
- 8 large prawns
- 250 g (8 oz) cod or other firm-fleshed white fish, about 1 cm (½ inch) thick
- Extra-virgin olive oil
- Sea salt
- Freshly ground black pepper
- Sprigs of flat leaf parsley, to garnish

1 Warm the olive oil in a medium sauté pan over medium heat. Add the onion and cook for 4–5 minutes, stirring occasionally, until soft and translucent. Add the garlic and chilli flakes and cook for 1 minute more, stirring occasionally. Stir in the remaining sauce ingredients, bring to the boil, then reduce heat and simmer for 10–15 minutes until the mixture reaches a sauce-like consistency. Break up any large tomato pieces with a spoon. Set aside.

2 Scrub the clams. Rinse the scallops under cold water and remove and discard the small tough side muscle. Peel and devein the prawns.

3 Prepare the grill for grilling over high heat (230–290°C/450–550°F).

4 Brush or spray the scallops, prawns and cod on all sides with oil and season with salt and pepper. Brush the cooking grates clean. Grill the scallops, prawns and cod over high grilling heat, with the lid closed as much as possible and turning once, until just cooked. The scallops and the cod will take 4–6 minutes. The prawns will take 2–4 minutes.

5 Meanwhile, bring the sauce to the boil, add the clams and cook, covered, for 3–4 minutes or until the clams open. Discard any unopened clams. Cut the cod into 2.5-cm (1-inch) chunks and add to the sauce. Then add the scallops and prawns. Warm the fish and shellfish briefly in the sauce, stirring occasionally.

6 Divide the fish and shellfish between four small soup bowls. Spoon some warm sauce on top, garnish with sprigs of parsley and serve immediately.

Marinated
SCALLOP
BROCHETTES
with Roasted Tomatillo Salsa

prep **30*** mins | bbq **10–14** mins | serves **4** | skill ★★☆

*marinating: 1 hour

Special equipment: 6–8 bamboo skewers, soaked in water for at least 30 minutes

MARINADE
- 3 tablespoons extra-virgin olive oil
- 1 teaspoon freshly grated lime zest
- 1 tablespoon fresh lime juice
- 1 tablespoon finely chopped garlic
- ½ teaspoon crushed red chilli flakes
- ½ teaspoon sea salt
- ¼ teaspoon freshly ground black pepper

- 24 large scallops, each about 40 g (1½ oz)

SALSA
- 1 small onion, cut crossways into 1-cm (½-inch) slices
- Extra-virgin olive oil
- 8 medium tomatillos, about 250 g (8 oz) total weight, husked and rinsed
- 1 poblano chilli
- 25 g (1 oz) fresh coriander, leaves and tender stems
- 1 garlic clove, crushed
- ½ teaspoon dark brown sugar
- ½ teaspoon sea salt

- 1 lime, cut into wedges, to serve

1 Whisk all the marinade ingredients together in a medium bowl.

2 Rinse the scallops under cold water. Remove and discard the small tough side muscle from any scallops that still have it. Place the scallops in the bowl with the marinade and toss to coat them evenly. Cover the bowl and refrigerate for 1 hour.

3 Prepare the grill for grilling over high heat (230–290°C/ 450–550°F).

4 Lightly brush the onion slices on both sides with oil. Brush the cooking grates clean. Grill the onions, tomatillos and chilli over high grilling heat for 6–8 minutes, with the lid closed as much as possible and turning once or twice, until lightly charred all over. Transfer the onions and tomatillos to a blender or food processor and place the chilli on a work surface. When the chilli is cool enough to handle, remove and discard the skin, stem and seeds. Add the chilli to the onions and tomatillos, along with the remaining salsa ingredients. Process until fairly smooth. Taste and adjust the seasonings if necessary.

5 Remove the scallops from the bowl and discard the marinade. Thread the scallops through their sides onto skewers so the scallops lie flat.

6 Brush the cooking grates clean. Grill the scallops over high grilling heat for 4–6 minutes, with the lid closed as much as possible and turning once, until just opaque in the centre. Serve warm with the salsa and lime wedges.

Grilled PRAWNS
with Smooth Mango-Lime VINAIGRETTE

prep	bbq	serves	skill
20* mins	2–4 mins	4–6	★☆☆

*marinating: 1 hour

MARINADE
- 4 tablespoons rapeseed oil
- 1 teaspoon sea salt
- 1 teaspoon garlic granules
- ½ teaspoon freshly ground black pepper
- ½ teaspoon ground cayenne pepper

- 750 g (1lb 8 oz) large prawns, peeled and deveined

VINAIGRETTE
- ½ ripe mango, roughly chopped
- 4 tablespoons rapeseed oil
- 50 g (2 oz) fresh coriander
- 1 spring onion, root end trimmed
- 1 tablespoon fresh lime juice
- 1 tablespoon rice vinegar
- 1-cm (½-inch) piece fresh ginger, peeled and chopped
- ½ teaspoon sea salt
- ¼ teaspoon freshly ground black pepper

1 Mix the marinade ingredients in a large bowl. Add the prawns and toss to coat thoroughly. Cover and refrigerate for up to 1 hour.

2 Combine the vinaigrette ingredients in a blender or food processor. Process for about 1 minute or until the texture is smooth and emulsified.

3 Prepare the grill for grilling over high heat (230–290°C/450–550°F).

4 Remove the prawns from the bowl and discard the marinade. Brush the cooking grates clean. Grill the prawns over high grilling heat for 2–4 minutes, with the lid closed as much as possible and turning once, until they are firm to the touch and just turning opaque in the centre. Serve the prawns warm with the vinaigrette.

Seared CALAMARI

with Chinese Leaf Slaw

prep **40*** mins — bbq **7–10** mins — serves **4** — skill ★★☆

* marinating: 45–60 mins

Special equipment: 8 bamboo skewers, soaked in water for at least 30 minutes

SLAW

- 4 tablespoons rice vinegar
- 2 teaspoons honey
- 75 ml (3 fl oz) extra-virgin olive oil
- 3 spring onions (white and light green parts only), thinly sliced on the diagonal
- 2 teaspoons finely chopped fresh ginger
- 1 teaspoon caraway seeds
- Sea salt
- Freshly ground black pepper
- 1 small head Chinese leaves
- 2 red peppers
- 7.5-cm (3-inch) piece cucumber

CALAMARI

- 3 tablespoons fresh lemon juice
- 2 tablespoons groundnut oil
- 1 tablespoon toasted sesame oil
- 1 teaspoon soy sauce
- 3 dashes Tabasco sauce
- 1 tablespoon finely chopped fresh coriander
- 1 teaspoon finely chopped garlic
- 1 teaspoon grated fresh ginger
- 1 teaspoon sea salt
- Freshly ground black pepper
- 750 g (1 lb 8 oz) calamari, each about 10 cm (4 inches) long, cleaned

1 Combine the vinegar, honey, 2 tablespoons of the olive oil, the spring onions, ginger, caraway seeds and ½ teaspoon each salt and pepper in a large bowl. Cut the Chinese leaves in half through the core. Cut the red peppers in half through the core, remove and discard the seeds and flatten the peppers with the palm of your hand. Brush the Chinese leaves and peppers with the remaining olive oil and season with salt and pepper.

2 Prepare the grill for grilling over high heat (230–290°C/450–550°F).

3 Grill the Chinese leaves and peppers over high grilling heat for 5–7 minutes, with the lid closed as much as possible, until nicely browned. Allow the vegetables to cool. Remove the core of the Chinese leaves. Cut the Chinese leaves crossways into 2.5-mm (⅛-inch) slices. Cut the pepper into 2.5-mm (⅛-inch) strips. Cut the cucumber into 2.5-mm (⅛-inch) slices. Add the Chinese leaves, peppers and cucumbers to the dressing and toss well. Cover and refrigerate for as long as 2 days. Bring to room temperature before serving.

4 Combine the lemon juice, groundnut oil, sesame oil, soy sauce, Tabasco sauce, coriander, garlic and ginger in a bowl and season with the salt and some pepper. With the tip of a sharp knife, lightly score the outside of the calamari (on both sides) in a cross-hatch pattern, but do not cut all the way through. Add the calamari to the bowl, cover with clingfilm and marinate in the refrigerator for 45–60 minutes.

5 Remove the calamari from the bowl and save the marinade. Thread the calamari on to bamboo skewers. Pour the marinade into a small saucepan and bring to the boil over a high heat; remove from the heat.

6 Brush the cooking grates clean. Grill the calamari over high grilling heat for 2–3 minutes, with the lid closed as much as possible and turning and brushing once with the boiled marinade, until just firm and white.

7 Serve the calamari immediately with the slaw.

FAJITAS
with Black Bean Salsa

prep
35*
mins

bbq
4–5
mins

serves
4

skill
★☆☆

* marinating: 30 mins

MARINADE

- 3 tablespoons fresh lime juice
- 2 tablespoons vegetable oil
- 1 tablespoon finely chopped garlic
- 1 teaspoon ground cumin
- 1 teaspoon sea salt
- ¼ teaspoon crushed red chilli flakes

- 4 skinless red snapper or sea bass fillets, each about 175 g (6 oz)

SALSA

- 500 g (1 lb) plum tomatoes, cored and diced
- 1 avocado, finely diced
- 140 g (4½ oz) canned black beans, rinsed and fully drained
- ½ red onion, finely diced
- 30 g (1 oz) fresh coriander, finely chopped
- 2 tablespoons fresh lime juice
- 1 tablespoon vegetable oil
- 1 tablespoon finely chopped jalapeño chilli, with seeds
- 1 teaspoon finely chopped garlic
- ½ teaspoon sea salt

- Vegetable oil
- 8–10 flour tortillas (25 cm/10 inches)
- ½ head romaine lettuce

1 Whisk the marinade ingredients together in a medium bowl.

2 Place the fish fillets in a large, resealable plastic bag and pour in the marinade. Press the air out of the bag and seal tightly. Turn the bag to distribute the marinade and refrigerate for 30 minutes.

3 Combine the salsa ingredients in a medium bowl. Season with more salt and lime juice, if liked.

4 Prepare the grill for grilling over high heat (230–290°C/450–550°F).

5 Remove the fillets from the bag and discard the marinade. Lightly brush or spray both sides with vegetable oil. Brush the cooking grates clean. Grill the fillets over high grilling heat for 3–4 minutes, with the lid closed as much as possible and turning once, until the fish begins to flake. Remove from the grill. Separate into large flakes with two forks.

6 Heat the tortillas over high grilling heat for about 1 minute, with the lid closed, without turning. Wrap in a tea towel to keep warm. Clean, core and cut the lettuce into thin, crossways slices. Let your guests assemble their own fajitas, piling the lettuce and fish on the warm tortillas and topping with the salsa.

Sicilian Stuffed
SWORDFISH
ROLLS

prep	bbq	serves	skill
35 mins	8–10 mins	4	★★☆

Special equipment: kitchen string or cocktail sticks

STUFFING

- 1 small plum tomato, deseeded and finely chopped
- 25 g (1 oz) breadcrumbs
- 1 tablespoon currants
- 1 tablespoon finely chopped flat leaf parsley
- 1 tablespoon finely chopped mint
- 1 teaspoon finely chopped oregano
- 1 teaspoon grated lemon zest
- 1 teaspoon finely chopped garlic
- ½ teaspoon sea salt
- ¼ teaspoon freshly ground black pepper

- 4 swordfish fillets, each 150–175 g (5–6 oz) and about 1 cm (½ inch) thick
- Sea salt
- Freshly ground black pepper
- Extra-virgin olive oil
- 4 lemon wedges

1 Mix the stuffing ingredients in a small bowl.

2 Place the swordfish fillets between two sheets of greaseproof paper and gently pound to a 5-mm (¼-inch) thickness. Season with salt and pepper. Place a quarter of the stuffing at one end of each fillet and roll it up. Secure each roll with kitchen string or a cocktail stick.

3 Prepare the grill for grilling over high heat (230–290°C/450–550°F).

4 Lightly brush the swordfish rolls with olive oil. Brush the cooking grates clean. Grill over high grilling heat for 8–10 minutes, with the lid closed as much as possible and turning once, until the fish is opaque throughout but still moist. Remove the string or cocktail sticks. Serve warm with the lemon wedges.

SWORDFISH STEAKS
with Watercress Sauce

prep 15 mins · bbq 8–10 mins · serves 4 · skill ★☆☆

SAUCE
- 1 large garlic clove
- 125 g (4 oz) watercress
- 25 g (1 oz) basil leaves
- 125 g (4 oz) soured cream
- 2 tablespoons mayonnaise
- ½ teaspoon grated lemon zest
- 1 tablespoon fresh lemon juice
- ½ teaspoon Worcestershire sauce
- ¼ teaspoon sea salt
- ⅛ teaspoon freshly ground black pepper

- 4 swordfish steaks, each about 175 g (6 oz) and 2.5 cm (1 inch) thick
- Extra-virgin olive oil
- 1 teaspoon finely chopped garlic
- ½ teaspoon paprika
- ¼ teaspoon sea salt
- ¼ teaspoon freshly ground black pepper

1 Chop the garlic very finely in a food processor. Add the watercress and basil and process until chopped. Add the remaining sauce ingredients and process until smooth. Pour the sauce into a small bowl. (If not using straight away, cover and refrigerate for as long as 24 hours.)

2 Prepare the grill for grilling over medium heat (180–230°C/350–450°F).

3 Lightly brush or spray the steaks on both sides with oil and then season evenly with the garlic, paprika, salt and pepper.

4 Brush the cooking grates clean. Grill the swordfish over medium grilling heat for 8–10 minutes, with the lid closed as much as possible and turning once, until the steaks are opaque in the centre but still juicy. Serve warm with the sauce.

TEQUILA SALMON

prep **20*** mins · bbq **9–11** mins · serves **4** · skill ★☆☆

*marinating: 30–45 mins

MARINADE

- 75 ml (3 fl oz) fresh orange juice
- 3 tablespoons extra-virgin olive oil
- 3 tablespoons tequila
- 1 tablespoon chopped fresh coriander
- 1 tablespoon finely chopped jalapeño chilli, with seeds
- 1 teaspoon garlic granules
- 1 teaspoon sea salt
- 1 teaspoon ground cumin

- 4 salmon fillets (with skin), each about 175 g (6 oz) and 2.5 cm (1 inch) thick

DRESSING

- 3 tablespoons extra-virgin olive oil
- 1 tablespoon fresh lime juice
- ½ teaspoon chilli powder
- ½ teaspoon sea salt
- ¼ teaspoon freshly ground black pepper

- 4 handfuls mixed salad leaves, 75–125 g (3–4 oz)
- 12 cherry tomatoes, halved
- 60 g (2 oz) fresh coriander
- 1 lime, cut into wedges, to serve

1 Whisk the marinade ingredients together in a small bowl.

2 Place the salmon fillets in a large, resealable plastic bag and pour in the marinade. Press the air out of the bag and seal tightly. Turn the bag to distribute the marinade, place in a bowl and refrigerate for 30–45 minutes.

3 Whisk the dressing ingredients together in a large bowl. Set aside until ready to serve.

4 Prepare the grill for grilling over medium heat (180–230°C/350–450°F).

5 Remove the fish fillets from the bag and discard the marinade. Brush the cooking grates clean. Grill the salmon, flesh side down, over medium grilling heat for 7–8 minutes, with the lid closed as much as possible, until you can lift the fillets off the cooking grate with tongs without sticking. Turn, skin side down, and finish cooking for 2–3 minutes. Slide a fish slice between the skin and flesh and transfer the fillets to serving plates.

6 Toss the salad leaves, tomatoes and half the coriander in the dressing. Divide the salad between the serving plates, garnish the fish with the remaining coriander and serve with lime wedges.

HALIBUT
with Grill-Roasted Lemon and Caper Dressing

prep 15 mins | bbq 10–14 mins | serves 4 | skill ★★☆

DRESSING
- 2 lemons, plus 2 extra to garnish
- 4 tablespoons extra-virgin olive oil
- 1 tablespoon capers, drained
- 1 tablespoon finely chopped chives
- ¼ teaspoon sea salt
- ¼ teaspoon freshly ground black pepper

RUB
- 1 teaspoon onion flakes
- 1 teaspoon finely chopped dill
- ½ teaspoon sea salt
- ¼ teaspoon freshly ground black pepper

- 4 halibut fillets, each 175–250 g (6–8 oz) and about 2.5 cm (1 inch) thick
- Extra-virgin olive oil

1 Prepare the grill for grilling over high heat (230–290°C/450–550°F).

2 Cut a 1-cm (½-inch) slice off both ends of each lemon. Cut each lemon in half lengthways. Lightly brush the cut sides of the lemons with 1 tablespoon of the oil.

3 Brush the cooking grates clean. Grill the lemons over high grilling heat for 4–6 minutes, with the lid closed as much as possible and turning once, until nicely browned. Remove the lemons from the grill and allow to cool. Set two aside for the garnish. Squeeze the lemons through a sieve into a small bowl. Discard the rinds and seeds. You should have about 1 tablespoon of lemon juice. Add the capers, then whisk in the remaining 3 tablespoons of oil to form a dressing. Whisk in the rest of the dressing ingredients and adjust the seasonings, if necessary.

4 Mix the rub ingredients in a small bowl.

5 Generously brush the halibut on both sides with oil and season with the rub. Grill over high grilling heat for 6–8 minutes, with the lid closed as much as possible and turning once, until the halibut just begins to flake when you poke it with the tip of a knife. Whisk the dressing one last time. Serve the fish warm with the dressing poured over the top.

SEARED SEA BASS
with Green Pea Sauce

prep
15
mins

bbq
5–7
mins

serves
6

skill
★★☆

SAUCE
- 25 g (1 oz) unsalted butter
- 1 small onion, finely chopped
- 250 ml (8 fl oz) chicken stock
- 125 g (4oz) frozen petit pois
- 2 teaspoons finely chopped tarragon
- 2 tablespoons double cream
- ½ teaspoon sea salt
- ⅛ teaspoon freshly ground black pepper

- 6 skinless sea bass fillets, each about 175 g (6 oz) and 2.5 cm (1 inch) thick
- Extra-virgin olive oil
- 1 tablespoon finely chopped tarragon
- ¾ teaspoon sea salt
- ¼ teaspoon freshly ground black pepper
- 250 g (8 oz) cherry tomatoes, cut into medium dice

1 Melt the butter in a medium saucepan over a medium heat. Add the onion and cook for 2–3 minutes until tender but not brown, stirring occasionally. Add the chicken stock. Raise the heat to high and bring to a vigorous boil. Add the peas and cook for 1–2 minutes until just tender. Pour into a blender and add the tarragon. With the lid of the blender off, process for 1–2 minutes until very smooth. Clean the saucepan and return the sauce to it. Add the remaining sauce ingredients, mix well and simmer for about 5 minutes, stirring occasionally, until it reaches a sauce-like consistency.

2 Prepare the grill for grilling over high heat (230–290°C/450–550°F).

3 Lightly brush the fish fillets with oil. Season with the tarragon, salt and pepper.

4 Brush the cooking grates clean. Grill the fillets over high grilling heat for 5–7 minutes, with the lid closed as much as possible and carefully turning once, until the flesh is opaque in the centre.

5 Meanwhile, reheat the sauce. Spoon some sauce on each plate, place a fish fillet in the middle and scatter the tomatoes over the top. Serve warm.

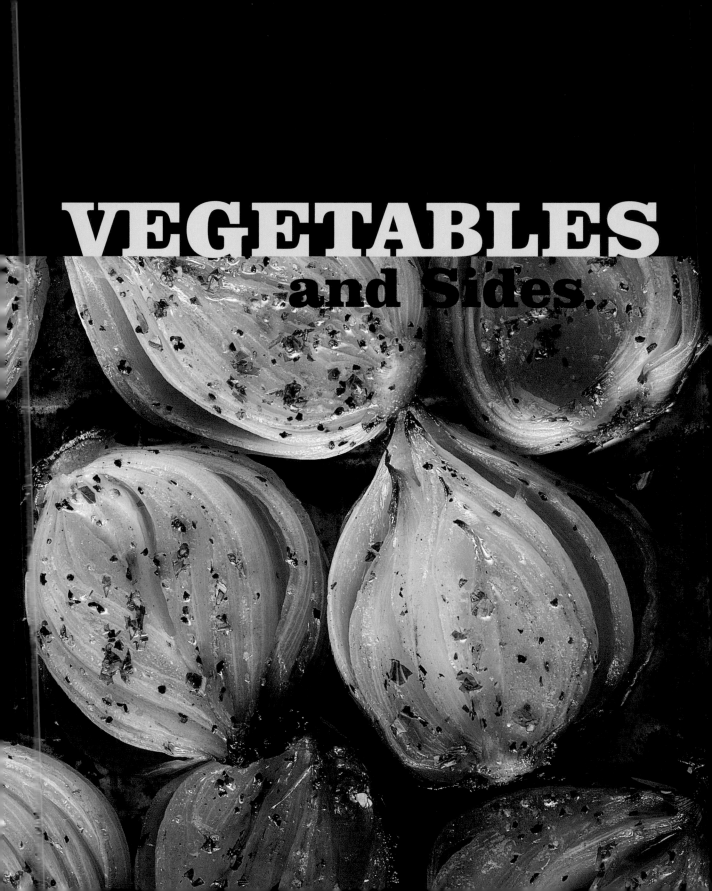

VEGETABLES
and Sides

Couscous-Stuffed TOMATOES

prep 45 mins   bbq 5 mins   serves 4   skill ★★☆

- 4 large ripe tomatoes

STUFFING
- 50 g (2 oz) quick-cooking couscous
- 75 g (3 oz) feta cheese, crumbled
- 6 kalamata olives, pitted and finely chopped
- 1 tablespoon extra-virgin olive oil
- 1 tablespoon finely chopped dill
- 1 tablespoon finely chopped basil
- ¼ teaspoon finely chopped garlic
- Sea salt
- Freshly ground black pepper

1 Cut a 1-cm (½-inch) slice off the top of each tomato; reserve the tops. With a small knife cut around the inside of the fleshy part of the tomato (do not cut through the bottom of the tomato) to within 1 cm (½ inch) of the skin. With a teaspoon, scoop out the tomato flesh, leaving about 1 cm (½ inch) of flesh attached to the skin. Discard the juice and seeds to make room for the stuffing. Turn the tomatoes, cut side down, on a plate lined with kitchen paper to drain while you prepare the stuffing.

2 Bring 5 tablespoons water to the boil in a small saucepan and add the couscous. Stir to combine. Cover and remove from the heat. Allow the couscous to absorb the liquid for about 5 minutes. Fluff the couscous with a fork and transfer to a medium bowl. Add the remaining stuffing ingredients, including salt and pepper to taste, and stir to blend. Spoon the stuffing into the tomatoes. Replace the tops.

3 Prepare the grill for grilling over medium heat (180–230°C/350–450°F).

4 Grill the stuffed tomatoes over medium grilling heat for about 5 minutes, with the lid closed, until the tomatoes are blistered and the cheese is melted. Carefully remove from the grill with a fish slice. Serve warm.

Bacon, LETTUCE

and Grilled Tomato
SALAD

prep
20
mins

bbq
6–7
mins

serves
4

skill
★☆☆

Special equipment: perforated grill pan

- 250 g (8 oz) thick-sliced bacon rashers, cut into bite-sized pieces
- Extra-virgin olive oil
- 1 small shallot, finely chopped
- 1½ tablespoons sherry vinegar
- 1 teaspoon finely chopped thyme
- ¼ teaspoon sea salt
- ⅛ teaspoon freshly ground black pepper
- 500 g (1 lb) cherry tomatoes
- 1 large crusty sandwich roll, cut in half lengthways
- 1–2 round lettuces
- 2–3 spring onions (white and light green parts only), thinly sliced

1 Cook the bacon in a large frying pan over medium heat until crisp. Using a slotted spoon, transfer the bacon to kitchen paper, reserving the bacon fat. Add enough olive oil to the bacon fat to make 6 tablespoons.

2 Mix the shallot, vinegar, thyme, salt and pepper in a small bowl. Whisk in the bacon fat/oil mixture in a steady stream to make a dressing.

3 Prepare the grill for grilling over medium heat (180–230°C/350–450°F).

4 Lightly coat the tomatoes with some of the dressing. Grill the tomatoes in a preheated, perforated grill pan over medium grilling heat for 5–6 minutes, with the lid closed as much as possible, shaking the basket wearing an insulated mitt or oven glove to turn them, until their skins begin to char and crack. Wearing the insulated mitt, carefully remove the vegetable basket from the grill and pour the tomatoes into a bowl.

5 Brush the cut side of the roll with some of the dressing and grill over medium grilling heat for about 1 minute, with the lid open and without turning, until toasted. Remove from the grill and cut into large croutons.

6 Arrange the lettuce leaves in a serving bowl. Add the tomatoes with their juices and the croutons among the lettuce leaves. Whisk the dressing one more time and spoon some over the salad (you may not need all of it). Top with the bacon and finish with the spring onions. Serve at room temperature.

German
POTATO
SALAD

prep
- 40 -
mins

bbq
-23–32-
mins

serves
4–6

skill
★☆☆

- 1 large red onion, cut crossways into 1-cm (½-inch) slices
- 3 tablespoons extra-virgin olive oil
- 1 kg (2 lb) waxy potatoes, each about 5–7.5 cm (2–3 inches) in diameter, scrubbed
- ½ teaspoon sea salt
- ½ teaspoon freshly ground black pepper

DRESSING
- 250 g (8 oz) bacon, rashers cut into 2.5-cm (1-inch) pieces
- 2 celery stalks, cut into medium dice
- ½ teaspoon granulated sugar
- 5 tablespoons cider vinegar
- 25 g (1 oz) wholegrain mustard
- ½ teaspoon freshly ground black pepper
- ¼ teaspoon sea salt
- 75 g (3 oz) dill pickle, diced
- 25 g (1 oz) flat leaf parsley, finely chopped

1 Prepare the grill for grilling over medium heat (180–230°C/350–450°F).

2 Brush or spray both sides of the onion slices with 1 tablespoon of the oil. Brush the cooking grates clean. Grill the onion slices over medium grilling heat for 8–12 minutes, with the lid closed as much as possible and turning once, until tender. Remove from the grill and cut into 5-mm (¼-inch) pieces. Cut the potatoes into quarters and put them in a large bowl with the remaining oil, the salt and pepper. Remove the potatoes from the bowl and spread them in a single layer on the grate. Grill over medium grilling heat for 15–20 minutes, with the lid closed as much as possible and turning every 5 minutes or so, until tender inside and crispy outside.

3 Begin making the dressing while the potatoes are grilling. Cook the bacon in a 30-cm (12-inch) frying pan over medium heat for 8–10 minutes, turning occasionally, until crispy. Drain the bacon on kitchen paper. Pour off all but 3 tablespoons of the bacon fat in the pan. Add the celery to the pan and cook for 3 minutes. Add the sugar and cook for 2–3 minutes, stirring occasionally, until the sugar is dissolved and the celery is cooked through. Add the vinegar and 125 ml (4 fl oz) of water; cook for about 2 minutes, stirring occasionally, until slightly thickened. Reduce the heat to low. Add the mustard, pepper and salt, stirring until combined, and cook for 2 minutes. Remove the pan from the heat; add the bacon pieces and the onions, tossing to coat with the dressing.

4 Transfer the potatoes from the grill to a chopping board. Cut each potato quarter in half and place in a large serving bowl. Pour the hot dressing over the potatoes, mixing gently to coat. Add the pickle and parsley. Toss gently and serve warm or at room temperature.

Hand-Cut FRENCH FRIES
with Spicy Ketchup

prep
10
mins

bbq
11–12
mins

serves
4

skill
★★☆

- 4 tablespoons tomato ketchup
- ½ teaspoon chilli sauce
- ½ teaspoon balsamic vinegar
- 2 baking potatoes, each about 250 g (8 oz)
- 1 tablespoon extra-virgin olive oil
- 1 tablespoon finely chopped garlic
- ½ teaspoon sea salt
- ½ teaspoon freshly ground black pepper

1 Mix the ketchup, chilli sauce and balsamic vinegar in a small bowl. Set aside.

2 Scrub the potatoes under cold running water and dry thoroughly (do not peel). Cut lengthways into 1-cm (½-inch) slices, then cut the slices into 5-mm (¼-inch) wedges. Place the wedges in a medium bowl. Toss with the olive oil, garlic, salt and pepper.

3 Prepare the grill for grilling over medium heat (180–230°C/350–450°F).

4 Place the wedges on the grill, being careful not to let them drop through the openings. Cook over medium grilling heat for about 10 minutes, with the lid closed as much as possible and turning once, until golden brown. For extra-crispy fries, open the grill and cook for an additional 1–2 minutes, turning once.

5 Serve warm with the ketchup.

Garlic-Roasted POTATOES
on Rosemary Skewers

 prep - **15** - mins

 bbq **25–30** mins

 serves **4–6**

 skill ★★☆

- 500 g (1 lb) new potatoes, each about 3.5 cm (1½ inches) in diameter
- Extra-virgin olive oil
- 1 tablespoon finely chopped garlic
- Sea salt
- Freshly ground black pepper
- 6 sturdy rosemary branches
- 5 tablespoons balsamic vinegar

1 Cut the potatoes in half and then place them in a medium bowl. Add 2 tablespoons oil and the garlic. Season with salt and pepper.

2 Strip almost all of the leaves from the rosemary branches to form skewers, leaving some leaves near the slightly thinner end. Finely chop enough leaves to weigh 25 g (1 oz) and add them to the potatoes. Toss the potatoes to coat thoroughly with the oil and seasonings. Using the thicker end of each rosemary skewer as a point, thread the potato halves onto the skewers, dividing the potatoes equally.

3 Prepare the grill for grilling over medium heat (180–230°C/350–450°F).

4 Brush the cooking grates clean. Grill the skewers over medium grilling heat for 25–30 minutes, with the lid closed as much as possible and turning once or twice, until the skins begin to brown and crisp.

5 Bring the vinegar to a simmer in a small sauté pan over a medium heat, then reduce the heat until a few bubbles are just breaking through the surface. Cook at a slow simmer until almost 2 tablespoons remain. As it nears this amount, the vinegar will cling to the back of a spoon and it will coat the bottom of the pan when you rock it back and forth. The total cooking time will be about 10 minutes, but keep an eye on the vinegar. If it cooks too quickly or it reduces too much, it will turn bitter rather than sweet. Remove the sauté pan from the heat (the vinegar will continue to thicken as it cools). Pour enough olive oil onto a serving platter to form a thin layer. Sprinkle the oil with salt and pepper. Drizzle the warm vinegar over the oil. Place the skewers on the platter, turn the potatoes in the oil and vinegar and serve immediately.

MELTED ONIONS

 prep 10 mins **bbq** 1¼–1¾ hours **serves** 4–6 **skill** ★☆☆

Special equipment: large disposable aluminium foil roasting tray

- 6 onions (unpeeled), each 250–300 g (8–10 oz) (about the size of a tennis ball)
- 50 g (2 oz) unsalted butter
- ½ teaspoon sea salt
- ¼ teaspoon freshly ground black pepper
- 1 teaspoon sherry vinegar
- 1 tablespoon finely chopped flat leaf parsley

1 Fill a chimney starter to the rim with charcoal and burn the charcoal until it is lightly covered with ash. Spread the charcoal in a tightly packed, single layer across half of the charcoal grate. Let the coals burn down to medium heat. Leave all the vents open.

2 With the onions still in their skins, place them on the charcoal grate against the charcoal. Close the lid and cook the onions for 1–1½ hours, until very tender. Occasionally swap the positions of the onions for even cooking and turn the blackened skins away from the charcoal. When very tender, the onions will be blackened in spots all over and a knife blade will slide in and out of each onion as if it is a ripe peach. Some onions may take longer than others.

3 At this point, to finish cooking the onions, you will need to add more charcoal to the fire for medium heat.

4 Remove the onions from the grill and let cool completely. Carefully remove the skin from each onion, being careful to leave the root ends intact so they hold the layers of the onions together. Cut each onion lengthways through the stem and root ends.

5 When the fire is ready, put the cooking grate in place. Melt the butter in a large disposable foil tray over medium grilling heat (180–230°C/350–450°F). Carefully add the onions in a single layer and season with the salt and pepper. Using tongs, turn the onions in the butter to coat them.

134

6 Slide the pan over medium roasting heat and cook for 10–15 minutes, with the lid closed as much as possible and carefully turning the onions once or twice, until the onions are very tender and just beginning to brown. If desired, to keep the onions warm, cover the tray with foil and let the onions continue to cook over roasting heat for as long as 30 minutes. Wearing insulated barbecue mitts or an oven glove, remove the tray from the grill. Splash the vinegar and sprinkle the parsley over the onions. Serve warm.

WHISKY
Barbecue
BEANS

prep
30
mins

bbq
1½–2
hours

serves
12–15

skill
★☆☆

Special equipment: Dutch oven

- 4 bacon rashers, about 75 g (3 oz) total weight, cut into 1-cm (½-inch) dice
- 2 onions, cut into 1-cm (½-inch) dice
- 1 tablespoon finely chopped garlic
- 125 ml (4 fl oz) tomato ketchup
- 4 tablespoons black treacle
- 4 tablespoons mustard
- 4 tablespoons whisky
- 1½ tablespoons brown sugar
- 2 tablespoons Worcestershire sauce
- 3–4 dashes Tabasco sauce
- 2 x 875-g (28 oz) cans baked beans
- Sea salt
- Freshly ground black pepper

- Mesquite or hickory wood chips, soaked in water for at least 30 minutes

1 Cook the bacon in a large sauté pan over a medium heat for about 10 minutes, stirring occasionally, until crispy. Add the onions and garlic and cook for about 5 minutes until soft. Add the ketchup, treacle, mustard, whisky, brown sugar, Worcestershire sauce and Tabasco sauce. Bring to the boil, reduce the heat and simmer for about 5 minutes.

2 Prepare the grill for roasting over medium heat (180–230°C/350–450°F). Follow the grill's instructions for using wood chips.

3 Rinse and drain the baked beans and put them in a Dutch oven. Add the sauce from the sauté pan. Stir to combine thoroughly. Place the pan on the cooking grate over medium roasting heat, close the grill lid, and cook for 1½–2 hours. Season with salt and pepper. Serve warm.

with Spicy Asian Dressing

prep **10** mins | bbq **8–10** mins | serves **4** | skill ★☆☆

DRESSING

- 1–2 serrano chillies, deseeded and finely chopped
- 3 tablespoons soy sauce
- 2 tablespoons fresh lemon juice
- 25 g (1 oz) onion, finely chopped
- 1 tablespoon water

- 2 large rounded aubergines, each about 375 g (12 oz)
- Vegetable oil
- 1 teaspoon garlic granules

1 Combine the dressing ingredients in a small bowl.

2 Remove about 1 cm (½ inch) from both ends of each aubergine. Cut the aubergines crossways into 1-cm (½-inch) slices. Generously brush both sides of the slices with oil and season evenly with the garlic granules.

3 Prepare the grill for grilling over medium heat (180–230°C/350–450°F).

4 Brush the cooking grates clean. Grill the aubergine slices over medium grilling heat for 8–10 minutes, with the lid closed as much as possible and turning once, until well marked and tender. Place the slices on a platter in a single layer. Immediately spoon the dressing over the top. Serve warm.

Grilled ASPARAGUS

with Balsamic Syrup

 prep 5 mins

 bbq 4–6 mins

 serves 6

 skill ★☆☆

- 125 ml (4 fl oz) inexpensive balsamic vinegar
- 1 kg (2 lb) asparagus (40–50 spears), each about 1 cm (½ inch) thick at the stem end
- 4 tablespoons extra-virgin olive oil
- ½ teaspoon sea salt
- ¼ teaspoon freshly ground black pepper

1 If you plan to reduce the balsamic vinegar on an indoor cooker, turn on the extraction fan. The simmering vinegar creates a pungent aroma. Bring the vinegar to a simmer in a small saucepan over a medium heat, then reduce the heat until a few bubbles are just breaking through the surface. Cook at a slow simmer until about 4 tablespoons of vinegar remain. As it nears this amount, the vinegar will cling to the back of a spoon and it will coat the bottom of the saucepan when you rock it back and forth. The total cooking time will be roughly 10 minutes, but keep an eye on the vinegar. If it cooks too quickly or it reduces too much, it will turn bitter rather than sweet. Remove the saucepan from the heat and let cool to room temperature (the syrup will continue to thicken as it cools).

2 Prepare the grill for grilling over medium heat (180–230°C/350–450°F).

3 Remove and discard any tough, woody ends from the asparagus spears. Peel the ends of the asparagus, if liked. Lightly coat the asparagus with the oil and season evenly with the salt and pepper. Brush the cooking grate clean. Lay the asparagus across the bars on the cooking grate. Grill over medium grilling heat for 4–6 minutes, with the lid closed as much as possible, rolling the spears a couple of times and swapping their positions as needed for even cooking, until lightly charred and crisp-tender.

4 Arrange the asparagus on a platter or individual plates. If the syrup is stiff, warm it briefly over medium heat. Drizzle some of the syrup over the spears (you may not need all of the syrup). Season with more salt, if liked. Serve warm or at room temperature.

Ember-Roasted
SWEETCORN
with Latino Flavours

prep **15** mins

bbq **10–15** mins

serves **6–8**

skill ★☆☆

- 3 corn cobs, outer leaves and silk removed
- Extra-virgin olive oil
- Sea salt
- 2 x 425-g (14-oz) cans black beans, rinsed
- 3 tomatoes, roughly chopped
- 2 celery stalks, finely chopped
- 15 g (½ oz) fresh coriander, finely chopped

DRESSING
- 3 tablespoons extra-virgin olive oil
- Finely grated zest of 1 lime
- 1 tablespoon fresh lime juice
- 1 teaspoon finely chopped garlic
- ½ teaspoon ground cumin
- ½ teaspoon sea salt
- ¼ teaspoon freshly ground black pepper

1 Prepare the grill for grilling over medium heat (180–230°C/350–450°F).

2 Lightly brush or spray the corn cobs all over with oil and season evenly with salt. Brush the cooking grates clean. Grill the sweetcorn over medium grilling heat for 10–15 minutes, with the lid closed as much as possible and turning occasionally, until browned in spots and tender. Slice the kernels off the cobs into a large bowl. Add the black beans, tomatoes, celery and coriander.

3 Whisk the dressing ingredients together in a small bowl. Pour the dressing over the black bean mixture. Mix to coat the ingredients evenly. Serve at room temperature.

Red Velvet CAKE

 prep **45** mins

 baking **25–35** mins

 serves **6–8**

 skill ★★★

* plus cooling

Special equipment: two 23-cm (9-inch) cake tins, electric mixer or food processor

- 300 g (10 oz) granulated sugar
- 100 g (3½ oz) butter or margarine, softened
- 375 g (12 oz) plain flour
- 1 teaspoon bicarbonate of soda
- 1 teaspoon salt
- 1 teaspoon cocoa powder
- 250 ml (8 fl oz) buttermilk
- 2 large eggs
- 2 tablespoons red food colouring
- 1 teaspoon pure vanilla extract
- 1 teaspoon white distilled vinegar

ICING

- 500 g (1 lb) icing sugar
- 250 g (8 oz) cream cheese, softened
- 500 g (1 lb) unsalted butter, softened
- 1 teaspoon pure vanilla extract

1 Preheat the oven to 180°C (350°F), Gas Mark 4. Lightly grease and flour two 23-cm (9-inch) cake tins.

2 Using an electric mixer or food processor, cream the sugar and butter or margarine until light and fluffy, scraping down the side of the bowl occasionally.

3 Sift the flour, bicarbonate of soda, salt and cocoa powder in a large bowl.

4 Whisk the buttermilk, eggs, food colouring, vanilla and vinegar in another large bowl.

5 With the mixer or processor running on low, add the buttermilk mixture and flour mixture in batches, starting and ending with the buttermilk mixture. Mix just until the mixture is smooth.

6 Divide the mixture evenly between the prepared cake tins. Bake on separate oven shelves for 25–35 minutes until a skewer or knife blade inserted into the centre comes out clean. Halfway through the baking time, swap the position of each tin. When fully cooked, remove the tins from the oven and run a knife along the edges to free the cakes from the tins. Carefully invert the cakes and let them cool completely on wire racks.

7 Using an electric mixer or food processor, mix the icing sugar, cream cheese and butter on low speed until thoroughly combined. Increase the speed and mix until the icing is light and fluffy, then add the vanilla. Occasionally turn off the machine and scrape down the side of the bowl.

8 Put one of the cakes on a serving platter. Spread the icing about 1 cm (½ inch) thick. Place the second cake on top. Scoop the remaining icing out of the bowl and spread it over the top. Continue to spread it to the edges and down the sides of the cake. Serve at room temperature.

GRILLED FIGS
with Cherry Sauce
and Toasted Coconut

prep 20 mins

bbq 2–4 mins

serves 4

skill ★★☆

- 150 ml (¼ pint) double cream
- 75 g (3 oz) cherry jam
- 1 tablespoon fresh lemon juice
- 20 g (¾ oz) desiccated coconut
- 25 g (1 oz) unsalted butter
- 12 large ripe black figs, cut in half lengthways
- 4 mint sprigs

1 Combine the cream and jam in a medium saucepan over a medium-high heat and whisk to break up the jam. Bring to the boil, then lower the heat and simmer for 5–8 minutes, whisking often, until 125 ml (4 fl oz) remains. Add the lemon juice. Pour the sauce through a sieve into a small saucepan.

2 Spread the coconut in a single layer in a large frying pan over a medium heat and cook for about 5 minutes until lightly browned, stirring occasionally. Pour the coconut into a small bowl to stop the cooking.

3 Prepare the grill for grilling over medium heat (180–230°C/350–450°F).

4 Melt the butter in a large frying pan over a medium heat. Add the figs to the pan and coat them in the butter. Grill the figs, cut sides down, over medium grilling heat for 2–4 minutes, with the lid closed, until well marked and tender. Meanwhile reheat the sauce over a low heat.

5 Spoon the sauce on the plates. Arrange the figs on top. Sprinkle the coconut over the figs. Decorate with the mint. Serve warm.

LEMON
ITALIAN ICE
with Raspberries

prep
30*
mins

serves
6–8

skill
★☆☆

*plus 8 hours to freeze

- Grated zest of 2 lemons
- 350 ml (12 fl oz) fresh lemon juice (8–10 lemons)
- 200 g (7 oz) granulated sugar
- ¼ teaspoon sea salt
- 475 ml (16 fl oz) cold water
- 500 g (1 lb) fresh raspberries

1 Combine the lemon zest, lemon juice, sugar, salt and water in a medium saucepan and cook over a medium heat until the sugar is dissolved. Pour into ice-cube trays and freeze overnight.

2 Put six to eight cubes in a food processor to make one layer. Pulse until the mixture is grainy and fluffy. Transfer the fluffy ice to a freezerproof container and repeat the process with the remaining cubes. Store tightly covered in the freezer until serving. Remove from the freezer 10–15 minutes before serving. Spoon into dessert dishes with the raspberries and serve cold.

APPLES

GRILLED in Paper

prep **15** mins

bbq **10** mins

serves **4**

skill ★☆☆

- 2 Granny Smith apples
- 50 g (2 oz) dried cranberries
- 4 tablespoons pure maple syrup
- 2 teaspoons light brown sugar
- ½ teaspoon ground cinnamon
- 25 g (1 oz) unsalted butter

1 Quarter the apples through the core. Remove and discard the core, then cut each quarter into thin slices. Place the slices in a medium bowl. Add the cranberries, maple syrup, sugar and cinnamon. Stir to combine.

2 Cut four pieces of baking paper each 30 cm (12 inches) by 37 cm (15 inches). Spoon a quarter of the apple mixture into the centre of each piece of paper and dot with a quarter of the butter. Bring the two long ends of each paper together and fold them over several times to seal the top of the parcel. Twist the other two ends of the papers in opposite directions to close the parcel.

3 Prepare the grill for grilling over medium heat (180–230°C/350–450°F).

4 Brush the cooking grates clean. Grill the parcels over medium grilling heat for about 10 minutes, with the lid closed.

5 Serve in the paper or pour the apple mixture from each parcel into a separate bowl. Either way serve warm, with ice cream if liked.

Berry
BISCOTTI
CRISP

prep **15** mins | bbq **20–25** mins | serves **8** | skill ★☆☆

Special equipment: 23-cm (9-inch) pie dish

- 700 g (1 lb 7 oz) fresh blueberries
- 500 g (1 lb) fresh raspberries
- 2½ tablespoons brown sugar

TOPPING

- 30 g (1¼ oz) plain flour
- 25 g (1 oz) brown sugar
- ¼ teaspoon ground cinnamon
- ¼ teaspoon sea salt
- 25 g (1 oz) unsalted butter, cut into 1-cm (½-inch) pieces
- 25 g (1 oz) almond biscotti, finely ground
- 50 g (2 oz) toasted almonds, roughly chopped

1 Gently mix the blueberries, raspberries and brown sugar in a medium bowl. Spoon the mixture into a 23-cm (9-inch) pie dish.

2 Stir together the flour, brown sugar, cinnamon and salt in a medium bowl. Add the butter. Using your fingertips, break the butter into smaller pieces, coating them with the dry ingredients. Add the ground biscotti and toasted almonds. Stir to combine. Sprinkle over the fruit.

3 Prepare the grill for baking over high heat (230–290°C/450–550°F).

4 Brush the cooking grates clean. Cook the crisp over high baking heat for 20–25 minutes, with the lid closed, until bubbling and lightly browned along the edges. Allow to cool for 5 minutes.

5 Spoon into serving dishes while still warm.

VANILLA CAKE
with Cherries and Cream

prep **20*** mins

bbq **35–40** mins

serves **8–10**

skill ★★☆

* plus cooling

Special equipment: 23-cm (9-inch) cake tin (5 cm/2 inches deep), electric mixer or beater

CAKE

- 1 tablespoon unsalted butter
- 250 g (8 oz) plain flour
- 2 teaspoons baking powder
- ¼ teaspoon salt
- 125 g (4 oz) granulated sugar
- 3 large eggs, at room temperature
- 125 ml (4 fl oz) milk
- 75 ml (3 fl oz) rapeseed oil
- 2 teaspoons pure vanilla extract

- 625 g (1 lb 4 oz) ripe cherries, stoned and quartered
- 3 tablespoons granulated sugar
- 1 tablespoon fresh lemon juice
- 250 ml (8 fl oz) double cream

1 Grease a 23-cm (9-inch) cake tin (5 cm/2 inches deep) with the butter. Sift together the flour, baking powder and salt in a medium bowl.

2 Using an electric mixer or beater, whisk the sugar and eggs for about 5 minutes until the mixture is pale yellow in colour. Add the milk, oil and vanilla and whisk for 2 minutes more. Add the flour mixture and whisk until just combined, scraping down the side of the bowl. Pour the cake mixture into the cake tin. Spread with a spatula to even out, if necessary.

3 Prepare the grill for baking over medium heat (180–230°C/350–450°F).

3 Bake over medium baking heat for 20 minutes, with the lid closed. Rotate the tin 90 degrees for even cooking. Continue to bake for 15–20 minutes more, until a skewer inserted in the centre comes out clean and there is no jiggle in the centre of the cake. Let cool completely on a wire rack. Run a knife around the edge of the cake, making sure to run the tip along the bottom of the tin. Invert out of the tin on to a board. Invert the cake again on to a serving platter.

4 Mix the cherries, half the sugar and the lemon juice in a medium bowl. Allow to stand at room temperature for 5–10 minutes. Meanwhile whip the cream with the remaining sugar to stiff peaks. Slice the cake and serve with the cherries and whipped cream on top.

Marshmallow Sandwiches

prep
15*
mins

bbq
2–3
mins

serves
8

skill
★☆☆

*drying: 24 hours

Special equipment: 4 long bamboo skewers, soaked in water for at least 30 minutes

- Peel of 1 orange, with most of the white pith removed, cut into 5-mm (¼-inch) strips
- 425 g (14 oz) granulated sugar
- 16 plain biscuits
- 8 thin squares, each 5 cm (2 inches), good-quality dark chocolate
- 8 large marshmallows

1 Bring a small saucepan filled three-quarters with water to the boil. Add the orange strips, blanch for 2 minutes and then drain. Place 1½ tablespoons of the sugar in a small bowl. In the same saucepan, bring 475 ml (16 fl oz) water and the remaining sugar to the boil, stirring to dissolve the sugar. Reduce the heat to a simmer, add the orange strips and simmer for about 10 minutes, stirring occasionally, until tender. Drain the orange strips and quickly put them in the bowl of sugar, tossing them with a fork or tongs. Allow the orange strips to dry on a rack at room temperature for 24 hours.

2 Prepare the grill for grilling over high heat (230–290°C/450–550°F).

3 Place eight biscuits on a plate, setting a square of chocolate on top of each one. Add one or two pieces of candied orange peel to each piece of chocolate. Thread two marshmallows on to the end of each skewer. Hold the marshmallows just above the cooking grate over high grilling heat and turn slowly for 2–3 minutes until lightly browned.

4 Slide a warm marshmallow on to each square, placing the remaining biscuits on top. Gently press together and wait for about 1 minute until the marshmallows melt the chocolate slightly. Serve immediately.

Caramelized PEACHES

with Lemons and Blueberries

 prep
10
mins

 bbq
8–12
mins

 serves
4–6

 skill
★☆☆

Special equipment: large disposable aluminium foil roasting tray

- 4 large peaches, firm but ripe, halved and stoned
- 40 g (1½ oz) unsalted butter, cut into small pieces
- 1½ tablespoons dark brown sugar
- ½ teaspoon pure vanilla extract
- 75 g (3 oz) shop-bought lemon curd
- 2–4 tablespoons double cream
- 250 g (8 oz) fresh blueberries

1 Arrange the peaches in a single layer, cut sides down, in a large disposable foil tray. Scatter the butter pieces and sugar between the peaches. Add the vanilla to the tray.

2 Whisk the lemon curd in a small bowl with enough double cream to create a smooth, spoonable sauce.

3 Prepare the grill for grilling over medium heat (180–230°C/350–450°F).

4 Place the tray of peaches over medium grilling heat and cook for 8–12 minutes (depending on the size and firmness of the peaches), with the lid closed as much as possible and rolling the peaches gently in the butter mixture once, until the peaches are tender, warm and glazed. To keep the peaches warm, slide the pan over roasting heat and open the grill's lid. When ready to serve, slide the hot pan on to a roasting tray and move to a work surface.

5 Cut the peaches into quarters or smaller slices. Arrange in bowls with the blueberries. Serve warm with the lemon curd spooned over the top.

INDEX

GRILL ACADEMY™

Welcome to the Weber® Grill Academy™

The purpose built Weber™ Grill Academy™ is a dedicated barbecue cooking school which stays open all year round.

Learn the freshest and most imaginative culinary ideas on themed courses covering a wide range

of barbecue cooking techniques from the basic to the advanced. On each course you will grill, roast, bake and smoke the Weber® way and take home all the skills, styles and techniques you need to really impress your family and friends.

Gift vouchers